Advance Praise for *The Agile Church*

Dwight Zscheile's *People of the Way* invited us to focus more on following the way of Jesus than on maintaining established churches. Now Zscheile's *The Agile Church* gives us  can try on new ways of participating in (vation and experimentation. This hopeful to move away from seeing Church as an e: toward reconceiving the Church as a resu **mission of God.**

—*Ian T. Douglas, Ph.D.*
Bishop of the Episcopal Church in Connecticut

In a world of easy, follow-these-10-steps answers to critical questions of leadership, it so good to have a book like this. You have in your hand the reflective work of a theologian who is rooted in the local, everyday life of a parish congregation. He knows what it looks like to work in the midst of challenges that need agility and innovation. Dwight's is a wise book, grounded in a theology of God's active participation with our world. His work on innovation is a rare gift for pastors and church leaders wanting something rooted deeply in Christian imagination and scripture, not just one more trend.

—*Alan Roxburgh*
Author, pastor and founder of The Missional Network

Zscheile perceptively captures the moment the church faces and understands that innovation must be a way of life for churches in the next decades. Churches practicing his "traditioned innovation," in which they make "good mistakes," learn from them, and move on quickly, have a chance to bear vital witness. This is one of the most important books I have read in a long time.

—*Lovett H. Weems Jr.*
Distinguished Professor of Church Leadership,
Wesley Theological Seminary

While the future of church is unpredictable, it is also more exciting and bright. In an age when people are making choices about their faith, spirituality, and lives in unprecedented ways, our churches have the opportunity to be nimble, graceful, and creative. *The Agile Church* is an ideal guide for this journey.

—*Doug Pagitt*
Pastor of Solomon's Porch and author of Church in the Inventive Age

Dwight Zscheile lives in two worlds comfortably. He knows more about leadership than just about anyone, and he really understands the church. In this book, he has found the right topic. Every church that wants to thrive in the future will need to be agile, and Dwight Zscheile is just the right person to show us how.

—*Scott Cormode*
Professor at Fuller Theological Seminary, Pasadena, California

I love this book for several reasons. First, it is hopeful. We've had plenty of church deconstruction; we need a way forward, and Dwight provides great practical and biblical advice. Secondly, the book blends insights from all kinds of fields: church, business, culture, sports, and life! We are desperate for this kind of integrative thinking to move us out of our church silos. Finally, it's just a plain, good read: easy to grasp, interesting, and thought-provoking. It's a book I wish I had written.

—*Reggie McNeal*
Best-selling author and missional leadership specialist

Conversant with Silicon Valley, yet seasoned in good theology, Zscheile lays out what church innovation can and must be: communal, traditioned, and agile. For any church that feels like a deer caught in the headlights, *The Agile Church* offers new hope and fresh direction.

—*David Fitch*
Professor at Northern Seminary, Bloomfield, Illinois,
and author of Prodigal Christianity

Dwight Zscheile's *The Agile Church* is an exceptional foray at the intersection of cultural studies, leadership theory, biblical narratives, and theological convictions, all with the assumption that God is an active agent in our neighborhoods and churches. Innovations toward new missional life are most likely when churches and their leaders exhibit certain characteristics and practices, and Zscheile provides clarity and on-the-ground stories to make this adventure more available for those ready to be participants in what the Spirit is already doing.

—*Mark Lau Branson*
Professor at Fuller Theological Seminary and author of Churches,
Cultures & Leadership *(with Juan Martínez)*

Dwight Zscheile has been exploring organizational, leadership, and innovation literature for some time. He is also passionate about the local church as it attempts to be a faithful theological enterprise dedicated to raising up leaders and engaging innovation. In this book, Dwight brings together the theological commitments of a pastor and scholar with important insights from sociology, and the church benefits from his work. This disciplined and practical volume is necessary for a missionary church.

—*Kyle J. A. Small*
Associate Dean and Associate Professor at
Western Theological Seminary, Holland, Michigan

The Agile Church

Spirit-Led Innovation in an Uncertain Age

DWIGHT J. ZSCHEILE

 Morehouse Publishing
NEW YORK

Unless otherwise noted, the Scripture quotations contained herein are from the New Revised Standard Version Bible, copyright © 1989 by the Division of Christian Education of the National Council of Churches of Christ in the U.S.A. Used by permission. All rights reserved.

Morehouse Publishing, 4785 Linglestown Road, Suite 101, Harrisburg, PA 17112

Morehouse Publishing, 19 East 34th Street, New York, NY 10016

Morehouse Publishing is an imprint of Church Publishing Incorporated.
www.churchpublishing.org

Cover design by Laurie Klein Westhafer
Typeset by Rose Design

Library of Congress Cataloging-in-Publication Data

A catalog record of this book is available from the Library of Congress.

ISBN-13: 978-0-8192-2977-9 (pbk.)
ISBN-13: 978-0-8192-2978-6 (ebook)

Printed in the United States of America

Contents

In memory of Jannie Swart, 1962–2014
Colleague and Friend

Acknowledgments

Over the past few years, I have had opportunity to travel frequently around the church to share in conversations with leaders in a variety of contexts struggling with how to thrive as Christian communities in the twenty-first century. Many of these leaders resonate deeply with the need to renew the church's identity in God's mission in a world in which the church is no longer culturally established. Yet they also wonder: What do we do next? What steps do we take? What kinds of practices will help us enter into deeper relationships with our neighbors? How do we learn what it means for us to participate more deeply in God's life in the neighborhood? How do we carry forward what is best from our past into a new world?

This book is written in response to those conversations. I am grateful to the many leaders who have shared their stories, yearnings, discoveries, disappointments, and hopes with me along the way. I hope this book may serve their journey in some small measure.

I give thanks especially for the local church where I serve part-time, St. Matthew's Episcopal Church in St. Paul, Minnesota, which has rooted my learning and research about agility in the particularities and possibilities of a specific community. Several leaders there shared valuable feedback on the book: Philip Boelter, Jeff Kidder, Terese Lewis, Blair Pogue, and Lisa Wiens Heinsohn.

Fourteen years ago, I first met Alan Roxburgh, who introduced me to the missional conversation. His thinking has been particularly formative for me on the themes explored in this book.

It was in several conversations with Scott Cormode that the impetus for this book took clearer shape. I'm grateful for the sources that he directed me to, and for his friendship and wisdom.

My colleagues at Luther Seminary have deepened and widened my understanding of these matters in so many ways. I am blessed to be part of a learning community seeking to adapt theological education for a time of disruption and change.

A number of people generously took the time to read and respond to drafts of this text: Eric Barreto, Tom Brackett, Mark Lau Branson, Cathie Caimano, Michael Chan, Scott Cormode, Ian Douglas, Scott Hagley, Timothy Hodapp, Cameron Howard, Stephen Lane, Jason Misselt, Brian Prior, Allison Read, Christian Scharen, Craig Van Gelder, and Steve Wiens. They have improved it significantly, though I take responsibility for any remaining errors.

It has been a pleasure to work again with my editor, Stephanie Spellers, always a wise and encouraging companion and friend.

Finally, I am most grateful for my wife, Blair, from whom I continue to learn so much about leadership and life, and for our son, Luke, an aspiring innovator.

Introduction

A Parable: Making Good Mistakes

Unlike my wife, I did not grow up playing tennis. She took years of lessons and played on her high school team. I played soccer and volleyball and surfed instead. When we married, she shared her enthusiasm for tennis with me and suggested we play together. I had played a number of sports; how hard could tennis be? I said sure. On the court, she graciously tried to give me a few pointers as it became rapidly evident to her that I could use some serious lessons. Yet, like many a novice facing the prospect of learning something new, I demurred. We still would occasionally play tennis together. I am enough of a natural athlete to have figured out how to hit the ball where it should go on the court—though not very elegantly or powerfully, needless to say.

A few years ago, my wife prevailed on me to take tennis lessons, using the wise strategy of conspiring with another tennis-playing woman in our church whose husband's game could use some improvement. We invited another mutual friend for strength in numbers. The three of us guys agreed to work with a local tennis instructor, Greg, for the summer. On the first day of lessons, Greg began by asking me to hit some balls with him. After a few tries, he shook his head and said, "No, no, no. Let's try this differently." He began to show me proper form. The problem is that when I tried this unfamiliar way of hitting, the ball was going over the fence and hitting cars in the street. (This is good in baseball, but not in tennis!) I felt rather embarrassed, as could be expected. But Greg enthusiastically affirmed me: "This is great! You're making *good* mistakes now." With some practice, the ball began to go where I wanted it to, with much greater power and accuracy than ever before. Previously, I was making the "bad mistake" of refusing to risk learning. The only way to growth involved making "good mistakes," even if they provoked in me no small degree of anxiety and embarrassment.

Learning and Growing in an Uncertain Age

This is a book about making good mistakes. Today's cultural environment presents churches with complex challenges for which there are no easy answers. Churches face dramatically changing cultural surroundings in which established patterns of Christian life and witness no longer connect with many people in the neighborhood. Forming and restoring community with these neighbors for the sake of Christian witness and service requires learning new ways of embodying and communicating the gospel. This work demands much from us and can seem daunting.

In the face of this challenge, many churches seem to be making the much bigger mistake of simply doing what they've always done, even if it isn't connecting deeply with their neighbors—and sometimes their own members—rather than risk learning and growing. The studies of religious affiliation, identity, and participation in American life today suggest a paradox: lingering, widespread Christian affiliation that often lacks depth, coherence, participation, and practice; rapid erosion of religious identification among younger generations; general openness to God and spirituality; and significant resistance to organized forms of religious community.[1] God's promises in Christ are steadfast, but the shape and future of the church in America is increasingly uncertain.

I know this uncertain future because I come from it. I grew up in a secular home without knowledge of Christian faith or practice. I regarded the churches in my town as religious clubhouses catering to their members; whatever happened inside them was a mystery to me. It would never have occurred to me that Christian community could be the answer to my search for meaning, purpose, identity, and belonging. The last place I would have brought my questions, dreams, and hopes was Sunday worship at one of those churches—nothing could be more intimidating! Were I to show up in many of those congregations, I would have been asked to migrate from my native culture into a "churchy" culture that would have been largely baffling to me. It may have been a culture perfect for fifty or a hundred years ago, but how it related to the gospel of Jesus and today's world would not have been at all clear.

Fortunately, God used ordinary disciples to meet me where I was and share the gospel with me in terms that I could understand. This witness was embodied in relationships and involved deep listening and acts of compassion. It was in cultural forms that made sense to me yet also challenged me to rethink my assumptions about life and the world. In the decades since then, I have been blessed to journey with a variety of different Christian communities, all of which have been deeply rooted in inherited traditions. Sometimes they have struggled to render those traditions accessible to their neighbors. Yet I have also seen them risk their lives to do so with creativity and love, making the good mistakes necessary to learn and grow. I will share some of their stories in the pages that follow.

I write this book from the perspective of one who knows what it is like to live without the freedom and grace of the gospel; to inhabit a story in which one must try to establish one's own worth, identity, meaning, and community rather than to receive them as a gift; to be caught in a cycle of estrangement and guilt with no hope of release. In my view, the stakes of the church's life and witness couldn't be higher—it is a matter of life and death for us personally, for our neighbors, and for the just and peaceful flourishing of the world. At the same time, my experience serving local churches has given me a profound appreciation for all that makes gospel witness in today's society difficult. I can understand why so many churches have a hard time connecting with their neighbors, particularly those who may speak different cultural languages. This is not easy work.

The church has spent a generation trying various technical fixes to address the decline of membership and institutional influence, while the trends have only continued and grown more widespread. For the most part, it has yet to address the deeper cultural currents at work, currents that undermine the assumptions and practices around which many churches have built their lives. Such assumptions and practices functioned well in embodying and communicating the Christian faith for earlier generations in many ways. Those elders comprise the majority of the membership of many congregations, and their faithfulness is to be praised. They have much to teach us. Yet if local churches are to have a future today, space must be made for new expressions of Christian life and witness to take shape in the native cultures of new generations and populations. *Such expressions must carry forward the best of earlier traditions*, embracing rather than forsaking the wisdom of the past. If, as Richard Foster observes, "Superficiality is the curse of our age,"[2] attempts to render Christianity relevant through stripping it of its depth, rootedness, and distinctiveness will not get the church anywhere.

This work of translating Christian faith and practice into new cultural vernaculars requires deep listening to God, to the tradition, and to neighbors. It requires prayer, patience, discernment, creativity, vulnerability, and risk. It pushes the church deeper into the central narratives of its faith. It is inherently uncontrollable and inevitably messy. It calls for new imagination (ways of seeing the world), habits, and practices. It is about learning and growing—in other words, *innovation*.

A Journey of Exploration

The innovation explored in this book is not one more quick-fix strategy for the church in order to reclaim some form of institutional success that it has lost. In the face of the more ambiguous, bewildering, and epochal cultural changes surrounding us, it is only natural for churches to look for one more technique or strategy to turn things around. If you're reading this book to find one, you will be disappointed.

Instead, I invite you on a journey of exploration as we approach agility and innovation in light of the church's establishment legacy and the Spirit's movement. In chapter two, we unpack some of the cultural shifts occurring in the twenty-first-century world, particularly those that touch on how people form religious and spiritual identity and community. We then turn in chapter three to tracing God's mission of forming and restoring community through ordinary, fallible people. Chapter four seeks to harvest from the world's most innovative organizations key insights and practices that can help the church learn from God and its neighbors as it embraces agility for the sake of witness and service. Chapter five names disciplines of a learning church, including addressing common obstacles to learning and change. Chapter six engages how church life might be organized to foster innovation, both within existing congregations and new church starts, as well as in theological education. The conclusion attends to a biblical journey in which loss and confusion turn to hope in the presence of the risen Lord. That hope affords us the courage to risk our lives for Christ and our neighbors.

Throughout this story, we will try to keep at the forefront of the discussion the person and power of the Holy Spirit, whose role in creating and restoring community is central to the biblical story and Christian teaching. The Holy Spirit is the agent of so much of the innovation that we find in the Bible—innovation that emboldens, encourages, and equips ordinary people for transformational witness. An agile church is, above all, a Spirit-led church. The Spirit of the Lord who hovered over the waters at creation, who liberated God's people from bondage in Egypt, who called judges and prophets to leadership, who rested upon Jesus as he proclaimed the year of Jubilee and healed the sick, who raised Jesus from the dead, who animated the early Christian community and led it out into mission—that very Spirit is doing new things in the church and world today. Our opportunity is to discover and participate in them.

Agility and Innovation

The word "agile" means "marked by a ready ability to move with a quick and easy grace."[1] Other definitions include "nimble," "adaptable," "flexible," "responsive," and "alert."[2] The root comes from the Latin verb *agere*, to act. It suggests agency, participation, dynamism. Many organizations today are recognizing the need for greater flexibility and responsiveness in the face of the accelerated pace of change that characterizes the twenty-first-century world. This means paying more attention to those outside the organization and watching carefully what is going on in the culture. It means listening to audiences and learning from them. It means being willing to adapt existing structures and patterns. It means clarifying who we are and what we are here for.

What would it look like for churches to embrace agility today? To attend prayerfully both to God and to a changing world? To adapt their lives in response to deep listening and relationships with those who are not part of them? To move with quick and easy grace, to be led by God in a dance? To identify and carry forward what is most life-giving and true, and to leave behind the baggage that gets in the way? Innovation and agility are in fact

1

nothing new for Christian disciples. They are integral to God's mission as described in Scripture, and they characterize many of the most vital moments of witness and service in the church's history. The long era of establishment for the church in Western societies rendered these dimensions of the church's life peripheral. Now is the time to reclaim them, which means revisiting the tradition in conversation with the realities of a shifting, pluralist culture and in dialogue with some of the best thinking on innovation from other organizations that know how to thrive in an agile world.

Contrasting Cultures

I grew up the son of a software engineer in and near Silicon Valley (even as it was just coming to gain that name). As an undergraduate at Stanford, I was surrounded by budding computer scientists who went on to found Internet companies. When I became a practicing Christian as a young adult, I had a hard time relating this familiar culture of innovation and entrepreneurship to my experience of church. Christianity offered a welcome alternative to the materialism and competitiveness of Silicon Valley. The church must embody alternative ways of seeing and living in the world, if it is to be faithful. Yet I found myself struggling with the church's propensity to focus primarily inward on those already a part of it, to force newcomers to learn a foreign cultural language in order to participate (a language that had little to do with the uniqueness of the gospel), and to fail to connect with people in my generation and diverse neighbors in the wider community.

The fact is that most churches—like most organizations generally—are not designed for innovation.[3] If you were to ask most people what words come to mind when they think of "church," I suspect few would offer "innovative." For churches focused on trying to survive in an increasingly inhospitable cultural environment, the concept of innovation can seem intimidating or overwhelming. It can seem a risky departure from how things have always been done—jeopardizing the allegiance of existing members who sustain the church. It can seem like one more task to add to already burdened leaders on the edge of burnout.

The examples of innovative churches celebrated in the media often operate in cultural contexts or with theological assumptions far removed from one's own. Most local churches are not called to become the next multisite megachurch or hipster emerging church. A different future awaits them to be discovered. It can be tempting to despair of the capacity of ordinary local churches to learn, adapt, and grow creatively in ministry in order to connect with their neighbors. Yet the biblical narratives are all about God working through ordinary, fallible, often uncooperative people who only dimly grasp their place in God's story. God does not give up on us; the heart of the Christian story is God bringing life out of death. As we will see in the discussion that follows, innovation is a profoundly biblical and theological theme.

Organized for Establishment

There are good reasons why many churches do not feel equipped today to engage in practices of innovation for the sake of Christian witness and service. In the United States, Canada, and Western Europe, the church is the inheritor of a long legacy of cultural establishment in which Christian identity and practice were generally thought to be supported by the surrounding culture. For generations, the church didn't have to focus on learning from neighbors how to be in ministry with them. It could assume people would find the church (on its terms) if they were interested. The church had a clear role in society—to hallow life's transitions, to take care of its members, to be a source of moral uplift to individuals and society, to get people into heaven, and to enrich Western culture.

This legacy of establishment has many dimensions. To begin with, churches tend to assume that their neighbors know who Jesus is, what church is, what churches do, and how to differentiate between types of churches (all of which were a mystery to me growing up). We assume parents teach their children the Christian story and practices at home, which Sunday school reinforces. Yet many parents don't know the story or practices very well themselves. Worship is often organized with the assumption that people can place the fragments of Scripture that we offer them (for instance, in the lectionary) into the wider narrative arcs of the Bible in order to make sense of them. Yet the church often hasn't taught those narratives effectively.

When newcomers show up, the church often focuses on assimilating them as participants in a voluntary religious organization ("have you filled out a pledge card?") rather than concentrating first on introducing them to Jesus and his Way. Churches often create little space for their members to share their real struggles with understanding, believing, and living the faith in daily life without fear of being shamed. Instead, church leaders assume that what the church says is understood, believed, and practiced, which is often not the case. Evangelism is often understood as inviting people to church, rather than equipping disciples to offer credible witness to Jesus within their relationships and spheres of influence. Such witness assumes the capacity to articulate the Christian gospel in personal and accessible terms—something many of the church's members struggle to do.

The establishment legacy assumes the church stands in a posture of centrality and power in its wider community, with a privileged moral voice. The church takes stands on various issues with the assumption that people will pay attention and listen to it on matters of public concern. Yet over the past decade, what the wider society has heard about the church in the media has been one scandal, moral failing, and conflict after another. Credibility must now be earned in the face of widespread skepticism. Outreach and social ministry efforts have typically been approached in the establishment mode as benevolence, where resources or services are dispensed to the less fortunate, often at arms' length. The church often assumes it knows what is best for the neighbor without having to listen, learn, and receive from the neighbor first.

The central challenge facing churches today is rediscovering who they are in a society that has in many ways rejected Christianity. Christian community cannot be assumed; it must be cultivated intentionally, both within established congregations and with new neighbors. This work is not primarily a matter of secular strategic planning, where we envision what we want our church to be in five years and develop a plan to manage our way into that future. It calls for a much deeper theological and spiritual rediscovery that recognizes God's presence, movement, and calling as primary to its identity.[4] It invites the church into a different posture—a posture of learning, vulnerability, and creativity.

Scholars of innovation observe that in the face of complexity, organizations must have good conversations about assumptions.[5] Each church in its context is unique, and the assumptions shaping your church's life and witness may differ from those named above. Yet wherever it is, the church can no longer take the assumptions by which it operates for granted. In the face of significant cultural change and complexity, assumptions must be articulated and wrestled with. When they no longer fit where we are today, they must be revised and adapted, which requires holding the life and patterns of our churches lightly enough to change them for the sake of loving our neighbors in Christ.

Treasures New and Old

In Matthew's Gospel, Jesus concludes a teaching session on parables by saying, "Therefore every scribe who has been trained for the kingdom of heaven is like the master of a household who brings out of his treasure what is new and what is old" (Matthew 13:52). The church has innumerable treasures in its life and history. These include the Bible in all its rich and diverse witness; the sacraments; practices like prayer, service, hospitality, reconciliation, testimony, and Sabbath; stories of faith heroes through the ages; doctrine; liturgies and worship traditions; and art, music, and other creative expressions of the faith. Every local church has in its own history powerful stories of Christian vitality and witness particular to its place, local "saints" who embodied the gospel to their neighbors. Sometimes these are people we know; other times they are legendary members of previous generations. Typically they are ordinary people through whom God does extraordinary things.

To be a church leader today is to be like that scribe trained for the kingdom who brings forth treasures new and old. It is tempting, in the face of many churches' establishment legacy and the missionary dilemmas surrounding us, to think we can somehow start over from scratch or "reboot" the whole Christian enterprise as if it were a computer that had frozen up. We might assume that traditional churches had been rendered obsolete like old typewriters in a digital age. But that is not at all the case.

What is required today is *traditioned innovation*. Innovation must remain rooted in the riches of Christian wisdom and practice from other times and places in order to offer deep, sustaining, faithful gospel witness. Otherwise, it might instead be based on a leader's charisma, idealized notions of community life, or some media or technology fad. Such innovations typically do not last. Any community that survives over time must adopt regularized patterns of life together. This institutionalization need not become bureaucratic ossification that chokes off creativity and growth.

Innovation grounded in tradition is what God's people have always done. The Bible itself is a great compilation of diverse voices and stories in which God's revelation in history is interpreted and reinterpreted through changing circumstances. God brings forth what is new in the life of Israel and in the church always in relation to what has been. The church's history consists of the renewal and retrieval of stories, traditions, and practices amidst the dilemmas and difficulties of new moments.

Yet so much of the debate about church renewal today seems to operate in unhelpful dichotomies or romantic idealism. There are those who want to create an "Acts 2" church of perfect community, while paying less attention to the remaining chapters of that biblical book, which are full of messy conflict and persecution as the early Jesus movement is dispersed from Jerusalem in mission. Others skip right over centuries of church history in trying to return the church to a more pure emulation of Jesus through recovering a primitive model of apostolic leadership. They seem to have little use for existing congregations in their particularity and complexity. There are those who embrace the latest media technologies and consumer marketing strategies in order to distance themselves from any traditional form of church, only to fall prey to the cultural captivities underlying contemporary consumer and entertainment culture. Others resist innovative expressions of Christian community in the name of old establishment models, such as the geographical parish. Yet that form of church is clearly not connecting well with most people within the "parish" bounds. Being a church for the neighborhood demands adaptations in habits and language in order to speak to neighbors that many churches are unwilling to undertake.

In its own way, each of these approaches brings a fruitful impulse to the conversation. But they tend to frame the question as an either/or, tradition *versus* innovation. It must be a both/and. We are called to bring forth treasures new and old. The answer today is not to hold on to existing forms of church life and practice unyieldingly when they no longer function well, nor is it to jettison established patterns wholesale. It is a matter of careful discernment, the cultivation by Christian leaders of the treasures of the tradition and a community's life so as to invite people into life-changing discipleship and witness. It is also a matter of *translation*—recognizing that the gospel always comes embedded in cultural forms, and as the cultural context changes, the shape of the church's life and witness too must change.[6] This is the deep logic of incarnation.

The incarnation signifies God's definitive revelation to humanity in person—through a particular human life, lived in a particular culture, in deep continuity with God's revelation to Israel. Jesus embodies God's presence as the one in whom humanity is reborn (or, in the classical words of the tradition, *recapitulated*; Ephesians 2:15). In Jesus the old era of humanity ruled by sin and death is replaced by a new era (Romans 5:12–21). The old reign of estrangement, disobedience, and division in which we are all implicated becomes in the faithfulness of Jesus a new humanity reconciled and restored within a new community encompassing every culture, tribe, and nation. Paul writes, "So if anyone is in Christ, there is a new creation: everything old has passed away; see, everything has become new!" (2 Corinthians 5:17).

The incarnation is in this sense a definitive divine innovation—the renewal of a human nature grown old, corrupted, and alienated. The root of the term "innovation" is the Latin word *nova*, meaning "new." God the Creator continually authors new life and also continually renews the creation by transforming in the Spirit what has fallen away from true identity, purpose, and right relationship. The cross and resurrection of Jesus define this story of innovation as we see humanity redeemed from the powers of oppression, violence, torture, and death.

This book explores what it might mean to understand God's innovative activity in creation, in the covenant people Israel, in Christ, and in the power of the Spirit as disciples form and renew Christian community in a pluralist age. The conversation will encompass both church planting and innovation within established churches. The formation of new expressions of church in order to incarnate Christian witness and service faithfully with those not reached by existing churches is absolutely vital. At the same time, most churches already exist and have rich histories upon which to build in adapting their lives for the sake of connecting with new neighbors.

Rediscovering Our Identity as Learners

Innovation involves learning. Learning is not easy for any of us— it is risky. There is always the possibility—indeed, the likelihood— of failure. It exposes our lack of competence, mastery, and control. It is frequently uncomfortable. There are many good reasons why churches resist learning. Foremost among these is the prospect that learning will involve change, and change will involve loss. Many churches today are paralyzed or numbed by grief over the loss of their children, grandchildren, vitality, and influence. They struggle with the prospect of losing cherished customs or known patterns, even if doing so might be necessary to adapt the church's life to speak to younger generations and diverse neighbors.

Learning is also necessary for our growth. Ephesians 4:15–16 says, "But speaking the truth in love, we must grow up in every way into him who is the head, into Christ, from whom the whole body, joined and knit together by every ligament with which it is equipped, as each part is working properly, promotes the body's growth in building itself up in love." To be a disciple of Jesus is to be a student, learner, or apprentice in a community of mutual growth in love. It means collaborating together, using all the spiritual gifts with which God has equipped us. It also involves mutual support, accountability, and encouragement.

When we read through the biblical narrative, we find that Jesus's disciples had a lot to learn about what it means to follow him. As we will see in chapter three, most of the time they seem fairly clueless, even in the presence of Jesus himself. Peter represents both the boldness and fallibility of this group of disciples. After the ascension, the disciples are led by the Spirit into powerful witness across cultural barriers but are perpetually learning and discerning the depth and reach of the gospel. This unfolds through resistance, persecution, misunderstanding, imprisonment, and much apparent failure.

The presence of failure at the heart of these biblical narratives of learning to follow Jesus should not surprise us, as failure is integral to learning and growth. One of the mantras of Silicon Valley is, "Fail early to succeed sooner."[7] Innovators know that the path to success inevitably proceeds through failure—often many, many failures. What does this mean for Christian disciples accustomed to a church that seeks power, mastery, and control rather than vulnerability, openness, and learning in mission? What role does failure play in the Christian story?

At the heart of the gospel is an apparent failure that shocked Jesus's students (disciples)—the crucifixion. Nothing could be more disappointing to those who wanted Jesus to overthrow the Roman oppressors than his betrayal, imprisonment, torture, and execution at Roman hands. Crucifixion was the most shameful and painful way to die in Jesus's world. It is no wonder that Peter and the other disciples went back to their old life of fishing.

Yet it is precisely in the embrace of the worst of human circumstances that victory and renewal spring forth in Christ. We should hold the terms "success" and "failure" lightly in our discussion of innovation, as we recognize the profound paradox at the center of God's redemption of the world. What might seem to be "successful" in conforming to the world's expectations might be far removed from how God is in fact renewing the world in Christ through the power of the Spirit. From a Christian perspective, the greatest apparent failure of all—the cross—is the very means by which God's purposes are accomplished.

Questions for
Discussion

1. Share a story of a time when you personally risked making a "good mistake" by trying something new. What was that experience like?

2. Identify a moment in your congregation's life in which you tried and failed in connecting with your neighbors or with different populations and generations. What did that experience teach you?

3. What in your congregation's current life represents a *traditioned innovation*—a new practice, custom, or initiative that is rooted deeply in what has gone before?

Faith and Spirituality
in a Fluid and Insecure Age

On a visit to the United States a few years ago, Martin Robinson, an English church planter and scholar, made a provocative remark to a small group of us gathered to think about mission in Western contexts. He said that he was always struck in America by how the conversation was primarily about *church*; in the United Kingdom, there isn't enough church left to talk about, so one must talk about *culture* instead. Martin was naming our American tendency to try to address the church's challenges by focusing on the church's internal life—its programs, worship, activities, strategies, etc.—without taking up the bigger question, which is what does it mean to be church in a culture that is increasingly hostile or indifferent to Christianity?

This question was first raised in a profound way by Lesslie Newbigin, a British missionary to India who retired to England only to discover that the "Christian" country that he had left decades earlier was no longer Christian in any meaningful sense. Newbigin began to wonder what a missionary encounter between the gospel and Western culture might look like, or in other words, *Can the West be converted?*[1] Newbigin's invitation to the church to approach late-modern Western culture with the eyes of a missionary remains one of the primary challenges before us.[2] The church tends to operate as if Western culture still supports Christian identity and practice. Yet this is increasingly no longer the case.

Religious Climate Change

The church in American society—as in other Western cultures—is facing what scholars of American religion such as Diana Butler Bass are describing as "climate change."[3] While local churches in different contexts are facing variable *weather* conditions—some more favorable than others—the overall religious climate is shifting decidedly against Christian participation and practice. Mark Chaves of Duke University puts it this way: "The evidence for a decades-long decline in American religiosity is now incontrovertible—like the evidence for global warming, it comes from multiple sources, shows up in several dimensions, and paints a consistent factual picture—the burden of proof has shifted to those who want to claim that American religiosity is not declining."[4]

The fastest-growing religious group in America today is those who claim no religious affiliation—a fifth of the U.S. population (up from 15 percent just five years ago), but a full third of those under age 30. Two-thirds of the religiously unaffiliated believe in God, but 88 percent say they are not interested in joining a religious organization. They perceive religious organizations as too caught up with money and power, too focused on rules, and too involved in politics.[5] Few Americans are actually so against religion as to proclaim themselves atheists, however. A majority of Americans continue to claim some kind of Christian affiliation, yet for a large number this does not translate into coherent Christian belief and practice or church participation.

It would be easy to assume that the decline in religious affiliation among younger generations reflects an established pattern from previous eras—people leaving church during college and early adulthood, only to return when they marry and have children. But today, marriage is happening later and later, if at all. A majority of U.S. households are no longer married households.[6] Furthermore, increasing numbers of young people have never been in church—there is no "returning" possible for them.

We must probe beneath these numbers in order to understand the major shifts taking place in the contemporary religious climate. Structures that nourished, supported, and encouraged Christian belonging and identity for generations are disintegrating in a twenty-first-century world of choice, fluidity, and insecurity. These shifts have deep roots, going back centuries in Western culture. They touch on basic questions of how we understand what it means to be human, how community is constructed, and what the nature and purpose of human life is all about.

It's All Up to You

If I were to summarize in one word the predominant shift affecting contemporary American religion and spirituality, it would be *choice*. So many aspects of human life that in previous eras were decided for us are now matters of individual discretion. Everything from what career to pursue, to where to live, to one's social and political affiliations, and even one's sexual identity is now a matter of ongoing discernment and self-discovery in ways unimaginable to previous generations. We live in a highly mobile world, where the stability provided by generations of extended family living in close proximity over time is now frequently disrupted by economic displacement, desire for new opportunities, or the seeking of different experiences far from home. The idea of "home" has itself become highly provisional—something that must be identified and constructed (if it exists at all) rather than inherited as a touchstone of who we are.

The shape of American families is dramatically changing with the delay and decline of heterosexual marriage (even as it is being expanded for same-sex couples), the prevalence of divorce, and the fact that many couples no longer see marriage as necessary or desirable for social respectability, parenting, or relational growth. Two generations have now grown up in homes where divorce is as likely to be a reality as intact marriages. Families are now scattered across the country or the globe, and while technology makes communication easier, it offers different levels of relational formation, nurture, and identity than those provided by regular in-person contact. Many people find themselves more or less on their own.

This fluidity of community renders human relationships far different than in many times and places in human history. Life in most societies has been shaped by a web of relationships not of one's own choosing—extended family, in-laws, neighbors, work colleagues, and social connections that derive from one's inherited place in a community. Sociologist Anthony Giddens uses the phrase "pure relationships" to describe how, in the modern world, people form ties with others primarily for the instrumental value they think the relationship will bring.[7] In other words, we connect with people because we think they will meet our needs for intimacy or otherwise help us advance our interests. Of course, the reverse also then becomes possible—when we feel like relationships are not meeting our needs, we switch out of them. This applies to everything from friendships to jobs to marriage—and to church.

Amidst all this, our sense of identity has become highly fluid. The self is a project one works on over the course of one's life through a series of choices requiring endless self-reflection. Much of this plays out at the level of lifestyle. We are formed by a consumer marketing culture that has elevated brands far beyond claims of intrinsic usefulness toward higher aspirations of meaning and belonging. Nike no longer tries to convince consumers that its shoes function or are made better than competitors' shoes—it sells a myth of performance, transcendence, and celebrity ("Just Do It"). We are told that if we buy Apple products, we are joining a tribe of the hip and stylish distinguished from everyone else. Commercials often no longer show the product they're trying to sell—just the brand. Our identities are marked by the brands we acquire and display, which now carry dimensions of spiritual meaning once reserved for religion. Wholeness, belonging, redemption, fulfillment, and even ecstasy all lie in the products and experiences we buy—at least that is what we are told to believe. Marketers are filling the void left by the erosion of church, family, and other forms of community.

Identity has become something we create and perform publicly through consumer lifestyle choices. Sociologist Zygmunt Bauman says, "In our fluid world, committing oneself to a single identity for life, or even for less than a whole life but for a long time to come, is a risky business. Identities are for wearing and showing, not for storing and keeping."[8] We associate with various cultural tribes (NASCAR fans who drink Budweiser or Whole Foods shoppers who drive Priuses, for instance) through consumer choices, which we not only display on our bodies and through our homes and cars but also broadcast through social media. We cultivate an image of ourselves (quite literally) on Facebook, Instagram, and other platforms that allow us to present and continually revise a particular self to the world. Marketing databases track every click and purchase and segment us into an increasingly sophisticated array of consumer profiles. The "selfie"—taking a photo of oneself with a smartphone or mobile device—is the archetypal gesture of contemporary culture.

As America shifts toward a service and information economy amidst globalization, the workplace has become another sphere of ongoing self-invention. Stable jobs and career paths are becoming rare as frequent offshoring, downsizing, outsourcing, and other forms of disruption constitute the new norm. The pace of technological change remakes whole industries within the span of a few years. No one knows what lies ahead, and only the nimble and adaptable survive, which places tremendous pressure on everyone, especially those who lack the education or skills to keep up. While globalization brings potential for wealth creation and choice for those positioned to benefit from it, many others find themselves disadvantaged, disoriented, and displaced. For them, the promises of consumer choice and self-actualization lie increasingly out of reach as they struggle merely to subsist.

Massive unease lies below all this. With no fixed anchors of identity and belonging, there is little security. Life in late-modern culture requires a kind of denial or exclusion of the deeper questions of death, meaning, and purpose.[9] We are haunted by the threat of meaninglessness and obsessed with security (Department of Homeland Security, alarm systems, electronic surveillance, gated communities, etc.), because our way of life is profoundly insecure at a much more basic level. The individual self has become the ultimate reference point for human life, and if the self is a fluid and shifting construct that we are responsible for creating and remaking, life is a tenuous, fraught, and ultimately lonely journey. Economic shifts render the twenty-first-century world deeply insecure for almost everyone, even professionals who once assumed their education and expertise would assure them a place.

This insecurity has major implications for how we understand community. Bauman notes that "gone are most of the steady and solidly dug-in orientation points which suggested a social setting that was more durable, more secure, and more reliable than the timespan of an individual life."[10] Each generation must make up its own path and choose fellow travelers on it. Yet that path and its travelers are always changing. While the desire for community endures and is even accentuated, the forms in which community is expressed are inherently provisional because its basis no longer lies in established and enduring structures (neighborhood, extended family, vocation, church, synagogue, etc.). People associate because they share similar perspectives, desires, or needs, but those associations are always liable to be broken and remade. Bauman continues:

> Community of common understanding, even if reached, will therefore stay fragile and vulnerable, forever in need of vigilance, fortification, and defense. People who dream of community in the hope of finding a long-term security which they miss so painfully in their daily pursuits, and of liberating themselves from the irksome burden of ever new and always risky choices, will be sorely disappointed.[11]

In other words, contemporary society is haunted by yearnings for community and connection that the shape of contemporary life continually frustrates.

One of the results of this fluidity is a fragmentation of American society that results in the formation of cultural and social tribes who now increasingly live separately from one another. In *Coming Apart*, the social historian and political scientist Charles Murray tracks how America has become segregated by class much more profoundly than fifty years ago.[12] As wealth disparity has risen dramatically in the past decades, upper-class Americans have come to live, work, and travel in enclaves surrounded by people of their own education and income levels. They share a culture of achievement, luxury, power, and relative health and family stability that middle- and lower-class America finds out of reach. The elites are sealed off from their economically struggling neighbors as many of the shared elements and common spaces of American culture have collapsed and disappeared. According to Murray, America is disintegrating, with an elite class that is morally "hollow at its core" and failing to exercise its responsibility toward the common good, and a lower class facing a collapse of community, family, industriousness, and opportunity.[13]

Part of the complexity of modern life comes from the fact that we must now try to understand and meet new expectations, particularly around issues of responsibility, ownership, and authority both at home and in the workplace, as Harvard psychologist Robert Kegan describes. For instance, as workers, we are now expected to invent our own work; to be self-initiating, self-correcting, and self-evaluating; to be guided by our own visions; and to conceive of the organization as a whole rather than just seeing our own part.[14] He observes, "Because the modern world expects of each adult the capacity for personal autonomy and authority, the self is not only a laborer, it is an arena of labor (we 'work on ourselves'). The self itself becomes a project."[15] Kegan summarizes this reality in terms of *self-authorship*.[16] We have to write our own stories, rather than receiving stories that make sense of the world and our place in it. The stories and materials that the culture makes available to us to work with tend to be superficial. They tell us we can buy and consume our way to happiness, that technology can solve every ill, and that positive thinking will overcome adversity. They are profoundly inadequate in the face of human suffering, brokenness, oppression, and death.

A Narrowing of Purpose

How did we come to this place? The philosopher Charles Taylor traces a long arc of historical development in Western societies that shifts from a God-centered cosmos in the premodern era to one focused on the human self in isolation, centered on it own ends.[17] For people in the Middle Ages and Reformation periods, God was an unquestionable presence and reality, and human life was understood to center on loving and worshipping God for God's glory. God was a force to be reckoned with—powerfully involved in daily life, requiring awe (the "fear of the Lord" in biblical terms), respect, and obedience. In a world in which war, disease, and death were undeniable, uncontrollable, and often close at hand, faith, prayer, and religious piety were integral to the fabric of life.

Beginning in the late seventeenth and early eighteenth centuries, a shift occurred toward the idea that what we owe God is essentially the achievement of our own good. Rather than God's glory being the primary end, humanity became the focus as an end in itself. Grace (unmerited favor) was eclipsed by reason and discipline, by which humans can rise to the challenge of recognizing and realizing God's order for the world. Mystery recedes and religion becomes narrowed to moralism—working diligently through self-discipline to do the right thing, which is achievable without any particular reference to or assistance from God.[18]

At its best, this approach retained a moral obligation to love the neighbor.[19] The sociologist Nancy Ammerman calls it "Golden Rule Christianity."[20] It boils down to loving your neighbor as yourself, a kind of "ethical spirituality" that remains the common denominator among Americans of various religious and nonreligious persuasions today: "The one thing that almost everyone agrees on, however, is that real spirituality is about living a virtuous life, one characterized by helping others, transcending one's own selfish interest to seek what is right."[21] You don't need God to practice ethical spirituality, however, and in fact many humanists and atheists are as committed to it (and good at it) as religious believers.

In the late twentieth century, a shift away from the moralistic understanding of human flourishing began to take hold. Having lost reference to a higher reality that humans should love or obey, human solidarity increasingly began to fade from the picture too. What remains is an understanding of human life and purpose centered on self-actualization and enjoyment, or as Miroslav Volf describes it, "experiential satisfaction."[22] The horizon and scope of human purpose have been reduced to the lifelong pursuit of a series of individually gratifying experiences, largely without any deeper framework of citizenship, virtue, or the common good. Other people matter mainly in that they serve our own quest for satisfaction. Volf says, "For religious people, this applies to God no less than human beings. Desire—the outer shell of love—has remained, but love itself, by being directed exclusively at the self, is lost."[23] That is, in the view of many people even God exists primarily to satisfy our individual desires.

"Expressive individualism" has become the predominant understanding of human life and purpose in contemporary Western societies, in which people are encouraged to find their own way, discover their own fulfillment, or do their own thing.[24] As Taylor notes, we live in a world with a "super-nova" of spiritual possibilities, an endless series of paths and options to try over the course of one's life. The criteria are no longer what religious identity, beliefs, or practices one might have inherited from one's family, but what seems most satisfying to the self in its pursuit of authenticity and actualization. There is no particular reason to abide long with any one faith tradition, practice, or community if it seems not to be meeting one's needs. British sociologist Grace Davie puts it this way:

> In Europe as well as America, a new pattern is gradually emerging: that is a shift away from an understanding of religion as a form of obligation and towards an increasing emphasis on

consumption or choice. What until moderately recently was simply imposed (with all the negative connotations of this word), or inherited (a rather more positive spin) becomes instead a matter of personal inclination. I go to church (or to another religious organization) because I want to so long as it provides what I want, but I have no obligation either to attend in the first place or to continue if I don't want to.[25]

From Family to Restaurant

Stefan Paas, a church planter working among secularized young people in Amsterdam, has found that it is fairly easy to get people to attend introductory classes on Christianity or even worship, but very difficult to get them to connect more deeply to his church or any other. He uses the metaphors of *family* and *restaurant* to describe the contemporary shift in religious community.

> People with a Christian background have been raised with the idea of the church as a family. Families stick together. People show up at parties and celebrations, even if they don't like them. That's what family members do for one another. They are connected by loyalty, duty, and (hopefully) love. Most other people, at least in Amsterdam, view church as a restaurant. It is a place where you go when you are in the mood—in other words, when you feel a spiritual need. You may like this particular restaurant very much, but this does not imply that you will return next week.[26]

Expressive individualism has turned religion and spirituality into an inner, private search, and churches are just one stop among many (if at all) for people on their journey. Paas writes:

> People no longer receive their identities from the outside (parents, family, nation), but rather construct them by looking

inside, at their "true selves." . . . In this context people tend to see religion as an instrument of personal development and no longer as something that one belongs to. They go to church like they go to a restaurant. Their quest can be very serious and deeply personal, but they will feel trapped and "inauthentic" whenever they are expected to submit their own desires and values to external authorities and moral expectations.[27]

The idea that one would surrender one's self to God or be held accountable to tradition, the Bible, or the practices and commitments of a particular faith community, is a foreign concept. After all, as Paas says, "'Community' is an ambiguous word for most modern people. They desire it and fear it at the same time. This is an age of 'light communities,' temporary and with many exit options."[28]

What Our Youth Are Telling Us

Extensive research has been conducted in the early twenty-first century about the religious attitudes, beliefs, practices, and affiliations of teenagers and young adults in America.[29] Known as the National Study of Youth and Religion, this research fills in the cultural picture more completely, and it is a challenging picture indeed. The youth in the study reflect the wider trends for religious identification in the American population in many respects— about half claim to be Protestant, about a quarter Catholic, about a fifth profess no affiliation, and the rest identify with Judaism, Mormonism, Islam, Hinduism, Buddhism, and scattered other faiths.[30] Yet when interviewed, a common theme emerged across a majority of the youth: with some exceptions, religion just wasn't that important and consequential to their lives.

Contrary to popular belief, the majority of American teenagers are not particularly rebellious in their religious identity, rejecting the faith of their families. Most indicated that their parents (and parents' churches) shaped their religious beliefs. They view religion positively overall, as a generally benign force for good, a nice thing. This perspective is even held by most nonreligious teens. However, when asked to explain or articulate their religious beliefs, those professing Christian affiliation largely struggled to do so.[31] What they described was something quite far removed from traditional Christian teaching. The researchers named it "Moralistic Therapeutic Deism," and it will sound familiar against the backdrop of the discussion above.

In Moralistic Therapeutic Deism, religion is instrumental—it exists to help individuals be and do what *they* want, not to make individuals change to adhere to God's teachings or calling. "For most U.S. teenagers, religion is something to personally believe in that makes one feel good and resolves one's problems. . . . God is treated as something like a cosmic therapist or counselor, a ready and competent helper who responds in time of trouble but who does not particularly ask for devotion or obedience."[32] Religion is about making people nicer (so that they treat others better) and making individuals feel better about themselves. American teenagers don't see religion as necessary for either of these things, however, so it becomes just an individual lifestyle choice that one can just as easily do without and live a good life.[33] Kenda Creasy Dean, one of the researchers, writes, "Teenagers tend to approach religious participation, like music and sports, as an extracurricular activity: a good, well-rounded thing to do, but unnecessary for an integrated life."[34]

Religion has been reduced to a minor aid to self-improvement—hardly a matter of life and death. No wonder so many young people (and older adults) have little use for it. At one point in American history, belonging to a church offered the promise of social prestige, respectability, and vital civic connections. It was a sign of community citizenship or ethnic or class identity. Since that is no longer the case in many places, people find it increasingly easy to walk away or diminish their participation. With so little at stake, why put up with the burdens and complexities of a religious organization when you can spend Sunday morning reading a spiritual book at Starbucks or watching an inspirational talk by Joel Osteen on TV? Why deal with those difficult people at church, have to serve on some committee, make a pledge, or otherwise be inconvenienced when life is already stressful and demanding enough as it is?

This reduction in the scope and relevance of religion is made possible in part because contemporary Western culture tends to understand "spirituality" as the immaterial dimension of human life—just one aspect alongside work, family, recreation, shopping, volunteering, etc. The ideal is a "balanced life" in which these dimensions are in harmony. Of course the challenge is that if you have a job in today's economy, you are working harder than ever (productivity has risen with a smaller workforce). The pace of life has sped up, and time seems in short supply. So spirituality becomes something that fits into the gaps, especially when one is distressed or perhaps feels an impulse to do some good. Church is just one more voluntary service organization, of which there are many offering the opportunity to do good, often more efficiently and with fewer obligations. If people increasingly see church as unnecessary to meet their spiritual impulses or needs, no wonder it gets eclipsed or abandoned. We must note, of course, that from a Christian perspective this view of spirituality represents a profound distortion. Christian spirituality is about *life in the Holy Spirit*, which encompasses all that we are and all that we have, including our bodies and material lives.

One of the reasons for the emergence of Moralistic Therapeutic Deism is the fact of religious pluralism in American life. Young people have been taught that tolerance, or getting along with others different from you, is a supreme value. It is not surprising that teachers, parents, and other authority figures would stress this given the complexity of difference that coexists in the United States today. Just as with civil religion fifty years ago, which fostered a common, generic belief in God in American culture in the face of the atheist threat of communism, Moralistic Therapeutic Deism serves as a lowest-common-denominator faith that everyone can adhere to.[35] The problem is that it covers over otherness rather than acknowledging or engaging it. It offers no grounds for bringing genuine difference into right relationship.

The sobering reality is that our youth are reflecting back to us precisely what we have somehow taught them—a superficial, accommodated version of Christianity. Kenda Creasy Dean says:

> The problem does not seem to be that churches are teaching young people badly, but that we are doing an exceedingly good job of teaching youth what we really believe: namely, that Christianity is not a big deal, that God requires little, and the church is a helpful social institution filled with nice people focused primarily on "folks like us"—which, of course, begs the question of whether we are really church at all.[36]

Christian Smith, a lead researcher in the National Study of Youth and Religion, writes, "Christianity is either degenerating into a pathetic version of itself or, more significantly, Christianity is actively being colonized and displaced by a quite different religious faith."[37] The church has at times actively fostered this by minimizing the distinction between its identity, life, and practices and the world's. This minimization has happened either as a legacy of cultural establishment or in the name of contemporary "relevance." The church has embraced therapeutic sermons, secularized its life and language, and turned its pastors into counselors catering to private inner needs or business executives with marketing plans. It has sometimes reduced the Bible to a toolkit for having a good marriage or being successful.

In order to try to reverse declines in membership, it has said that it is easy to become a Christian, when of course Jesus says quite otherwise.

I was struck recently when my son came home from elementary school and made a comment about how all religions are basically the same. That is not a message he has ever received at home from his parents (both of us are pastors). We have tried diligently since his birth to help him understand the uniqueness of the Christian story and how it differs from other religions and philosophies. While stressing respectful engagement with those of other traditions, we have had many conversations about what is at stake in the gospel. Yet the wider culture in which he is immersed is so powerfully formative that it threatens to overwhelm what we have sought to teach him.

An Impoverished Imagination

In reflecting on how contemporary culture has colonized the church, we must recognize that culture is not just something we examine from the outside; it lives within us. It is how we experience and interpret life. It is the story we live in, the air we breathe. One of the most important insights of the past century is that all of life is interpreted—we make sense of our experiences through stories, categories, forms, and practices from the culture(s) in which we participate. Often, we are unaware of these assumptions and influences and don't think or talk much about them. Yet they are constantly reinforced by daily interactions. We get along with others in part by conforming to them. They constitute the matrix by which we negotiate daily life.[38]

For many people in Western societies today, that shared imagination (as diversely expressed as it may be) relegates God and the church to insignificance. Even as people participate in Christian worship, adult education, youth groups, service trips, and other patterns of organized faith, the cultural framework within which they are interpreting those experiences has the effect of domesticating the Christian story into *its* categories and assumptions. Those religious experiences are simply resources to draw on in constructing a sense of identity and purpose within the constraints of an individualistic trajectory of self-discovery.

The sociologist Robert Wuthnow uses the term "tinkering" to refer to this phenomenon in his research on younger adults in America. "A tinkerer puts together a life from whatever skills, ideas, and resources that are readily at hand."[39] Wuthnow suggests that this improvisational self-compilation and self-definition of spirituality is the predominant mode for younger adults early in the twenty-first century. There is significant freedom to choose from a wide range of possibilities, whether from traditional religions or alternatives, and there is no particular need to integrate them into any real coherence. Wuthnow observes that young adults are probably more influenced by their friends than by the formal teachings of religious organizations.[40]

Contemporary culture has shaped people's imaginations such that they struggle to connect their personal stories and the world's story to God's story. The large study of youth and young adults referenced above isn't the only evidence of this. Nancy Ammerman and her colleagues recently conducted significant research on how ordinary Americans of a variety of religious affiliations or no affiliation interpret their lives spiritually. For participants, there are many places of everyday life largely untouched by any hints of transcendence or spirituality, such as neighborhoods in which people live or how people spend money. She says, "What people do in their households, at work, taking care of their health, or engaging in politics is largely narrated as a story whose characters are defined by routine roles and whose actions are aimed at practical ends"—without any sense of connection to the transcendent.[41]

As referenced above, the primary way Americans talk about faith in daily life is in terms of ethical spirituality, or serving others and being a good person. Yet people who participate in church are little different from those who don't on this front. On average, religiously active people were no less socially engaged in serving their neighbors than unaffiliated people, but no more so.[42] The picture that emerges is of a spirituality focused on narrow dimensions of life, understood largely in moralistic terms, and irrelevant to much of daily life in the world. In other words, God is understood to help people get through certain parts of their days, but for many Americans God doesn't otherwise seem to make much of a difference.

Ministry in Cultural Headwinds

How has the church responded to this sea change in the culture? Largely by trying harder at old patterns. Churches think that if they just get the right leader, she or he will rescue us, bring in new people, or fix the problem of institutional decline and irrelevance. They try to market the church better, spruce up websites, perhaps put out a nice new sign by the road proclaiming "All are welcome." The church seeks to improve worship and programming a bit. All of this has no material impact on the underlying situation. People aren't looking to be welcomed into a church like they once were. The church can do worship beautifully and brilliantly, and it isn't going to be accessible or meaningful to most of its neighbors.

More pointedly, the church rarely listens long enough to its unchurched or disconnected neighbors to learn how the church might meaningfully connect with their hopes, dreams, struggles, and spiritual yearnings. In shame and grief, it doesn't ask its children or grandchildren why they no longer participate in church or how church might have to change to speak to them. Come to think of it, the church rarely listens to its own members' spiritual struggles and ways of seeing the world in order to find out whether the gospel is meaningful for them and making a difference in their lives.

Instead, churches tend to operate with untested assumptions. For instance, liturgies and prayers typically narrate worship as if people were experiencing it as an opportunity to give God glory and praise, when the culture forms them to come looking for a spiritual boost of divine intimacy and some encouragement to be a better or nicer person. The church asks people for pledges to support it as if this is an accepted and understood obligation for members. For older generations shaped by a culture of duty (particularly the World War II generation), that often works. But for younger generations, obligations and duties are things to be cast aside in the pursuit of "authenticity" and "freedom." Making a voluntary financial pledge to anything out of duty—especially a sacrificial one—is a strange concept. Church life is organized around various committees, on which people are expected to serve as a mark of their faithfulness and discipleship. But often the relationship between serving on a committee and learning and practicing the Way of Jesus is unclear (to say the least!). Most people in today's world don't need one more thing in their schedules; if anything they need help simplifying and focusing their lives.

The church wonders why regular worship attendance is now being redefined for many churches as once a month, rather than once a week. Leaders are disappointed at the eroding levels of commitment and think that if they can only invite people more effectively they will respond just as they used to. The church uses traditional language of "vocation" to refer to people's "callings" in daily life with the assumption that they know the Caller and are listening for a call. Yet this conception simply doesn't function for many people. They don't experience daily life and work as sacred or meaningful by any stretch. The church wonders why, when faced with a choice between a Sunday morning youth sports tournament or church, families often choose the tournament. If we were to ask them, they would probably say it is because they find more meaning, community, and moral formation in the sports team than in church.

I'm still haunted by a young man in a church I served some years ago. David (not his real name) was a computer programmer who would attend church only occasionally with his wife and young son. She was actively involved in church and an important volunteer, even while working full-time. But I found it easier to get David to come into the church office to work on the computers during the week than to participate in any religious functions. I learned over time, however, that David was a member of the local volunteer fire company. He spent hours training, serving, and hanging out with the fire team. The fire team was his primary community, not church. As I reflect on it, I can understand why. The fire company had a clear mission that was undoubtedly a matter of life and death for the whole community. They had strong disciplines that shaped their life together, with real accountability. Being part of the fire team involved hard work and sacrifice, but also high levels of engagement and trust—in a fire, their lives depended upon one another. They were bound together deeply in a shared pattern of life and service.

Somehow, we in the church had never asked that kind of commitment of David. We had failed to communicate the life-or-death stakes of the gospel in a way that he could understand. Thank God David was serving in the fire company—I wouldn't want church to interfere with this important service to the wider community. But why couldn't our church call him to share in its own transformational community focused on God and oriented toward the common good? The fire company may have met many of David's needs for meaning, belonging, and purpose, but only to a point; the gospel goes much deeper, addressing ultimate realities of suffering and death that any firefighter will eventually encounter firsthand.

It's Not Your Fault

It would be easy, in all this, to lay the blame upon ourselves as leaders. We watch the church's vitality, relevance, and institutional strength erode before our eyes, and we feel responsible. We think that if we only worked harder, preached better, brought more energy, met people's needs more, or found the right program or technique, things would turn around. If you're thinking those thoughts and find yourself discouraged, I have a simple message for you: *this cultural shift is not your fault.* There is nothing you could have done or can do to reverse the cultural changes that have come upon us. It is much bigger than any of us.

Many church leaders I know are frustrated, bewildered, grieving, and anxious for their livelihoods, all for good reason. Many congregations exhibit the classic stages of grief: denial, anger, bargaining, depression, and acceptance (with the early phases most common).[43] It is easy to despair or not know where to turn. We look enviously at churches that seem to be successful and wonder where we went wrong and what they're doing right. We try to adopt their programs and plans, as if that would solve things for us. We get bitter at the sports leagues that schedule their activities to conflict with times once held sacred for church. We feel betrayed when members depart or refuse to commit to deeper participation in the church. All of this is perfectly understandable given the circumstances. But it won't address the basic challenges facing us. For that, we have to focus elsewhere and embrace a quite different approach. We must turn toward the story of God's engagement with the world.

Questions for
Discussion

1. What signs of religious climate change do you notice in your family and neighborhood?
2. How has your church tried to respond?
3. What might these cultural shifts mean for your church's relationship with its members? What about its neighbors?

Forming and Restoring Community in a Nomadic World

Beginning Where People Are

At the heart of Christianity lies a simple but distinctive claim: God meets us where we are. Some philosophies and spiritual paths focus on helping people pray, work, meditate, or climb up to God. This often entails an escape from the grittiness of mundane life, toward a pure, ethereal realm far removed from daily struggles. But Christianity reverses this. God in Christ enters into human existence fully, in an ordinary family, in vulnerability, humility, and poverty, in the flesh, under seemingly inauspicious circumstances (an insignificant town of an occupied people suffering under a global empire). God moves into the neighborhood, into the very spaces of ordinary struggle and survival that seem to be so emptied of the sacred for many Americans today.

When God meets us where we are, we're invited to see our lives and world through different eyes. We see that what once seemed godforsaken is where God is in fact present and at work. We see that at the heart of God's purpose is the creation and restoration of communities of justice and mercy in which all may flourish. If God meets us where we are, the church too is led by the Spirit to meet its neighbors where they are in a posture of learning, reciprocity, and vulnerability. This involves claiming the freedom to translate God's Word into particular cultures in particular times and places so that all may hear, see, and know the hopeful and life-giving gospel story amidst the contrary stories of our world. We come to recognize leadership as less about managing people into the plans, programs, and visions leaders create, and more about accompanying people on the Way of Jesus as we help them reinterpret their lives and world in light of the gospel.

In order to understand this movement more deeply, we must reenter the biblical narratives and trace how God meets people where they are and calls them into the adventure of God's mission. These narratives reflect the complexity and ambiguity of human life as they testify to a God who compassionately bears with people even amidst their sometimes poor and tragic choices. We must rehear the stories of imperfect, doubting, unfinished humans like us being entrusted by God with seemingly impossible callings and promises—futures into which they typically stumble rather than achieve with competence and mastery. In, through, and sometimes in spite of their very humanity, God sets about restoring the world. We inhabit the same story today.

Created for Community

The Bible begins with a story of God ordering the cosmos in creativity and love. The culmination of the creation is humanity, made in God's image and given the sacred vocation to care creatively for the earth so that it might flourish (Genesis 1:26–30). The distinction between male and female represents the difference in relationships that is the basis for unity and collaboration. God builds diversity into the basic fabric of the cosmos as a predicate for community. Yet it is not long before the story goes on to describe community fractured by self-centeredness and mistrust. Such is the human story—created for community, yet prone to go our own ways, to seek our own ends rather than others', to turn inward rather than to live interdependently in trust with God and one another.

The painful fracturing of community continues with murder in the next generation (Cain and Abel) and the widespread distortion of human relationships leading up to the Flood (Genesis 6). God calls Noah and his household as the ones through whom human community will be reconstituted under an unconditional promise: God will never again destroy the whole earth. But even Noah succumbs to drunkenness and shame (Genesis 9).

As the generations continue in this narrative, the human tendency to huddle together in sameness out of fear of the world finds expression in the Tower of Babel, an attempt by people to make a name for themselves (Genesis 11:4). Rather than receiving an identity from God as gift and blessing—the pattern built into creation—humans resist God's call to spread out across the world and be fruitful. God scatters them to frustrate this fundamental perversion of the nature of human community: our identities are gifts from our Creator and are grounded in trusting God's calling for our lives. They lie in our being sent into the world. We don't have to write our own stories—we belong in God's story.

Calling a New Community

From these primordial stories, archetypal in their sweep and power, the narrative enters a new phase with the calling of Abraham and Sarah. These two receive their call in their seventies, having endured childlessness, a source of significant shame in that culture. God's call to them is simple, but not easy: "Go from your country and your kindred and your father's house to the land that I will show you. I will make of you a great nation, and I will bless you, and make your name great, so that you will be a blessing" (Genesis 12:1–2). They are told to leave what is familiar and to trust that they will have descendants and settle in a land already occupied by someone else. They are nomads for the sake of God's promise to bless the world, chosen for the purpose of a greater good. Through them God will form a new community. On the face of it, it is not a very likely outcome.

How does their journey go? Like most biblical stories of people following God's call, it is circuitous and complicated. There is a famine in the land to which God sends them, so they must sojourn in Egypt. Abraham jeopardizes the promise by passing Sarah off as his sister, and she is taken into Pharaoh's harem. Having been extricated from that fiasco, the wandering continues, with God's pledge of land and descendants still far off. Abraham vacillates between trust in God (accounted to him as righteousness in Genesis 15:6) and doubt (fathering Ishmael with Hagar, Sarah's slave, among other things). Almost twenty-five years pass by, and still no child for Sarah and no land. God persists in calling, but Abraham and Sarah meet that call with laughter, and understandably so! They are almost one hundred years old. Nothing in this story seems to make sense in the world's eyes.

The journey continues. You would think that Abraham would have learned his lesson about passing Sarah off as his sister, but he does it a second time—even after God's promise of a son through her has been repeated and confirmed. Finally, Isaac is born. Yet Abraham is tested with a call to sacrifice the very son who embodies God's promise. The story of Abraham and Sarah, patriarch and matriarch of faith, is a strange one indeed. It is a story fraught with ambiguity, demanding great patience from them (and

God), and involving both cooperation with God's call and apparent resistance, doubt, and failure. It is a story of risk—being willing to get up and go from what is familiar—and new learning at every step of the way (even when the lessons need to be repeated). Churches, especially those full of aging members, sometimes think God's call has passed them by; the story of Abraham and Sarah should invite us to imagine otherwise.

We could explore in detail the next couple of generations of people through whom God works (Isaac, Rebecca, Jacob, Leah, Rachel, Joseph), and we would find more of the same—people often choosing selfishly and failing to grasp clearly God's calling for them. We would see cheating (Jacob steals his brother's birthright) and human trafficking (Joseph is sold into slavery). We would see God somehow working through it all. It is tempting to read the biblical narrative with the assumption that the people whom God calls opt readily into God's mission to bless the nations and carry out their roles like heroes. But, as Allen Hilton reminds us, the opposite is actually true.[1] Those figures the Bible lifts up as central to God's work in the world are commonly inward-looking, uncooperative, and doubting, and have to be pushed through experience to learn what God's purposes are. There is a pedagogical process underway—an adventure of learning that proceeds through trial and error in real time and in the concrete circumstances of daily life.

Moses is a great example of this. When God calls Moses in Exodus 3, Moses finds himself exiled into the hinterlands from the Egyptian household of privilege in which he was raised as an adopted son of Pharaoh. He has married the daughter of Jethro, a priest from another faith, and taken up shepherding Jethro's flock, not the most glamorous profession. Having murdered an Egyptian taskmaster, Moses must feel like an utter failure, exiled and marginalized. But God meets him there, in his daily life and work, in the very place of dislocation and despair. God's call knits them together in a common compassion—both of their hearts break for the suffering of the people. God sees in Moses much more than Moses can see. Moses's response to the call is one hesitation, refusal, and qualification after another. God persists and adapts, working with Moses as he is. The rest of the story is a process of growth and learning as Moses comes to live into the leadership God saw in him all along. Yet poignantly, Moses never makes it into the Promised Land.

Dislocation and Discovery

Liberation from Pharaoh's empire of slavery and oppression does not deliver the people of Israel directly into a place of security, prosperity, and peace, but rather into the wilderness. The wandering in the wilderness for forty years (long enough for a generation to die) is a space of spiritual transformation, learning, and communal re-creation. Having lived for generations in the structures, habits, and stories of slavery and empire, Israel must learn anew what it means to be God's people. Like their ancestors of faith, Abraham and Sarah, the whole of Israel becomes nomadic, inhabiting an in-between space of uncertainty, austerity, and transition.

The wilderness stories hold particular resonance for churches that find themselves displaced from settled patterns into an uncertain new environment. It would be hard to overestimate the formative power of the wilderness for Israel's identity. This new community that God is creating to bless the nations emerges not from the powerful, prominent, settled nations of the world, but from a bunch of former slaves. They don't know clearly this God who has liberated them and calls them to new life. Their path is not direct, clear, and predictable, but shifting, open-ended, and full of detours. They must learn how to trust in God's presence (symbolized by the pillar of cloud and fire), provision, and leadership without the established order of empire. It is no surprise that they revert and rebel. They murmur against God and their leadership. They pine for the food of Egypt rather than the lean manna that God provides, which spoils if you try to hoard it. They make idols out of gold, rather than trust in the living God.

There is no shortcut through the wilderness for God's people because it is precisely in the ambiguity and difficulty there that they learn how to be God's people. It is where their communal life (expressed in the Law received by Moses) takes shape, a way of life that distinguishes them from other nations as a holy people, a covenant community. It is where their imagination is renewed, where the colonizing stories of slavery give way to trust and dependence on the God of freedom.[2] The wilderness is a place of loss, hardship, and testing—a place no one really wants to be. It is a crucible where the old habits and patterns die and something new is born.

While it would be easy to see the crossing of the Jordan from the wilderness into the Promised Land as the end of this learning and formation process, it is hardly so. Entering the Promised Land brings all sorts of ambiguities and challenges for a people still prone to mistrust God and chase after idols. The books of Joshua, Judges, and 1 and 2 Samuel are full of violence and moments of profound anxiety, doubt, and fear. The people clamor for a king rather than recognize God as their ruler. A core lesson God's people struggle to learn throughout the Bible is to trust in God's power and leadership. Churches used to the cultural support of the establishment era find themselves wrestling with the same question—how do we recognize our life is utterly dependent upon God?

In the face of repeated threats and the fragmentation of their own community, God's Spirit raises up leaders and empowers people for action. This section of the Bible in particular is full of battle stories, often asymmetrical engagements where this band of former slaves goes up against established armies. They are complex and unsettling stories of God's power being demonstrated in the face of unlikely odds. The story of David and Goliath makes this point emphatically. Yet God's people continually revert to idolatry, abandoning their calling and identity. These stories again and again stress God's long-suffering love (in Hebrew, *chesed*) even and especially amidst human betrayal. They also highlight the Spirit's work of unifying and building up community.

Israel asks for a king and gets one. Yet these kings, including David and Solomon, under whom Israel establishes its own empire, bear all the marks of human frailty. Saul is a figure haunted by fears and confusion, even as he is anointed and called by the Spirit. David, the archetypal Israelite king, is not the obvious choice for the job by any stretch, and when he does assume his role, he commits adultery and rape with Bathsheba. The pattern should be clear by now: God chooses unlikely people with faults and flaws and, through their fragile humanity, works in the power of the Spirit. God stands in solidarity with those who suffer along the way.

Redescribing Reality

As the biblical story continues, Israel finds itself in a changed situation: rather than suffering under other empires, it can claim its own empire—for a little while at least. David's successors intermarry with foreign wives for the sake of political and economic gain, and in so doing compromise Israel's calling as a covenant community showing forth God's holiness to the world. This brings forth the prophets, who are raised up by the Spirit to tell a different story than the predominant narrative among the spiritual and political elite. During the period of the monarchy, Israel's prosperity often comes at the expense of its integrity. The poor and vulnerable (widows, orphans, resident aliens in particular) are exploited. Patterns of justice and mercy in faithful worship of God and in the ordering of human community are violated. God's people seem to forget who they are and what they're here for.

The work of the prophets, as Walter Brueggemann has so aptly argued, is to reinterpret the world in light of a God of freedom.[3] The prophets are called, sometimes from the margins and sometimes from the center, to speak public words of judgment and promise. These words critique the distortions of human community in the status quo. They remind the people of God's presence and power and their dependence upon God. They invite a renewed way of seeing reality in which God is at the center. In so doing, the prophets call the people to live into a story that they struggle to understand and embrace—a story in which God forms, leads, and calls them to a unique way of life in order to bless the world. As described in chapter two, many church members today struggle to interpret their lives in light of God's presence and movement.

Reading through the prophetic literature brings us face-to-face with politics—including the drama of nations contesting for power and control. Israel and Judah (during the period of the divided kingdom) face threats from larger and more formidable nations—the Assyrians and Babylonians, and their successors, the Persians, Greeks, and Romans. The question of security underlies these books of the Bible: Where is true security to be found? This major biblical theme of struggling to trust in the Lord of history rather than in human powers or false gods pervades the prophetic literature. It remains a key spiritual challenge for the church today.

The periods of exile in Assyria and Babylon represent another painful space of dislocation, austerity, transition, and learning for God's people. Exile was deeply traumatic, involving loss of everything familiar, including deeply held theological beliefs that God would indwell and protect the Jerusalem Temple and its leaders. If the predominant story was that God would bring the nations to Zion (Jerusalem) to worship the Lord, nothing could seem like a greater failure than being displaced from Jerusalem. Did this mean that the God of Israel was not as powerful as other gods? What was God up to in all this? Things weren't supposed to turn out this way. Where is God when circumstances don't turn out like we expect them to? Many churches struggle with this question now.

It is precisely in these spaces of greatest dislocation, pain, and confusion that prophets like Isaiah, Jeremiah, and Ezekiel tell a new story. When Jerusalem's elite assumes that their violent displacement into Babylon must be a quick and temporary aberration, God dictates a letter to the exiles through Jeremiah to tell them otherwise. The message is clear: put down roots, plant gardens, have children, get to know your neighbors, seek the flourishing of the foreign city into which God has sent you, for your own well-being depends upon its well-being (Jeremiah 29:4–7). As in the biblical wilderness, there is no quick escape from exile, because it is where God's people relearn what it means to be in relationship with God.

Living in exile is difficult, painful work. It takes place amidst colossal failure—being conquered by a foreign empire, being stripped of the institutional and material security upon which they had depended for generations. At root, it is about coming to see reality differently, changing one's assumptions about where and how God is active in the world. The prophets testify to God's ability to use even foreign kings (Nebuchadnezzar, Cyrus) for God's purposes. These are discomforting stories—upending our categorizations of the sacred and profane. The living God of history—the God to whom the Bible testifies—will not be domesticated.

The story we have been exploring so far is a story of God coming where people are, in their faithfulness, pride, weakness, vulnerability, doubt, and yearning. It is a story of God calling regular people, often the unlikeliest by human standards, and sending them to participate in God's creation and restoration of community in the Spirit. This sending has a nomadic character, epitomized by the call of Abraham and Sarah: "Go." It is a journey of displacement, more a wandering than a straight trip to a clear destination. It takes time—time in places God's people don't want to be. There is tremendous loss, surprise, provision, victory, and failure along the way. It is a journey of faith, meaning it is about coming to see, know, and follow God's presence, movement, and promises even when the evidence seems to the contrary.

Joining Up in Person

This story reaches its greatest depth in the life, death, and resurrection of Jesus. In Jesus, the God who calls, liberates, and wanders with Israel becomes nomadic in order to join us where we are in person. For the sake of forming and restoring community, the Word becomes flesh and lives among us (John 1:14). God moves into the neighborhood, into the particular and local, to bring us and all people into right relationship. As Mary's song (the "Magnificat") recognizes, the child to be born to her brings dramatic reversals to the entrenched powers of the world—powers Mary experienced acutely as a young woman in an occupied land. Jesus embodies the promise made to Abraham and Sarah so long ago (Luke 1:46–55).

Jesus's ministry in the Spirit begins with a call to see and act differently: "The time is fulfilled, and the kingdom of God has come near; repent, and believe in the good news" (Mark 1:15). The term "repent" (*metanoia* in Greek) means to change one's mind. As in the Hebrew Bible narrative explored above, God is continuously calling people into a new way of interpreting and experiencing the world—one of the primary needs facing the church in a secularized culture today. This is a recurrent theme in

Jesus's encounters with people, where he invites them to perceive reality differently—to have "eyes to see" and "ears to hear." This idea is a struggle for many, such as Nicodemus, who misinterprets Jesus's call to new life: "How can anyone be born after having grown old?" (John 3:4). The presence of God's reign (or kingdom) is not always obvious—it springs forth from what seems small and insignificant, like the mustard seed.

Jesus goes about forming a new community in the Spirit by meeting people where they are, such as Matthew at his tax collecting booth or Simon Peter and Andrew fishing. His ministry is fundamentally nomadic—a circulation around Galilee and its environs, leading toward Jerusalem—in order to connect with people where they are in their towns and villages. The disciples whom Jesus calls fit with the pattern established in the Hebrew Bible—they are ordinary people from a variety of walks of life, none particularly well-credentialed for this work.

Forming a Learning Community

Jesus's community of disciples is a fluid one, with the Twelve called to symbolize a reconstitution of the twelve tribes of Israel, key women in the inner circle, and larger circles of crowds who come and go. To be a disciple in the ancient context was to be a learner, apprentice, or student, not so much in an *informational* sense but in a *formational* sense. That is, following Jesus meant close observation of his actions in relationship, going where he went, staying where he stayed, sharing conversations, listening, and trying things out. It was about being formed into a new way of life—what came in the book of Acts to be called "the Way."

Jesus gave his students repeated opportunities to experiment with ministry, such as sending the Twelve (Luke 9) and the Seventy (Luke 10). These experiences build on time they've already had observing Jesus proclaiming the peace of the reign of

God, healing the sick, teaching, and engaging in public dialogue. Jesus sends them for these short-term engagements into places he himself intends to go (Luke 10:1). They are sent empty-handed to rely upon the provision of the people in the neighborhood, so they must trust and depend upon God and other people, without being able to impose their own will. They go with the very real possibility of refusal, which Jesus himself faced repeatedly. Not everyone in the neighborhood will share in the peace, but the peace is not lost even if the neighbors refuse it (Luke 10:6).[4]

Jesus's disciples engage in a learning process through his time with them that is fraught with misunderstanding, confusion, and even denial. Even as the disciples rejoice in their powerful experiences of healing and preaching, Jesus invites them into a deeper understanding of his identity and calling. This understanding includes teaching about the cross—subverting their expectations that Jesus would be a political messiah who would violently overthrow the Romans. Peter tries to talk Jesus out of it and is met with a stern challenge: "Get behind me, Satan! For you are setting your mind not on divine things but on human things" (Mark 8:33). Peter's imagination has yet to be renewed sufficiently to grasp what God is up to.

Peter embodies the ambiguity of discipleship in the Gospels—the stumbling into God's mission that we find in the Hebrew Bible. He is willing to leap out of the boat and attempt walking on water, but begins to doubt and sink (Matthew 14:28–31). He confesses, "You are the Messiah" (Mark 8:29) but doesn't really know what this means. He is as close to Jesus as any of the disciples, yet rashly attempts to use violence against the High Priest's slave when Jesus is arrested, failing to grasp the nonviolence at the heart of Jesus's Way (John 18:10–11). Most poignantly, Peter denies Jesus three times after his arrest (Matthew 26:69–75).

Even in the context of the Last Supper, the disciples argue about which of them was to be regarded as the greatest (Luke 22:24).

The male disciples all abandon Jesus at the crucifixion. In Mark's Gospel, they are never clear even to the end about who Jesus is; it is up to a Roman soldier to confess Jesus's identity: "Truly this man was God's Son!" (Mark 15:39). After the resurrection, Mary Magdalene and the other disciples struggle to recognize Jesus; she mistakes him for a gardener (John 20:15). Thomas's doubt is emblematic of what we find among the whole group of them. At the conclusion of Matthew's Gospel, as Jesus is about to send the remaining eleven out in the "Great Commission" to make disciples of all nations, "some doubted" (Matthew 28:17). In this sense, they are very like us.

How does Jesus respond to these struggles among his followers to see and behave clearly and faithfully? In a word: *gracefully*. Jesus does not shame or reject his disciples. Even when he must pointedly challenge a deep misunderstanding, such as Peter's distorted view of what it means to be the messiah, Jesus stays in relationship. He does not shun and turn his back on them. "Father, forgive them; for they do not know what they are doing" (Luke 23:34) encapsulates Jesus's posture of longsuffering patience, consistent with the steadfast love (*chesed*) of the God of Israel. When Peter and some of the other disciples had gone back to fishing, having given up on ministry in the aftermath of Jesus's crucifixion, Jesus shows up on the beach, where they are, and feeds them. He reverses Peter's three betrayals with three questions and callings: "Do you love me?" "Feed my sheep." "Follow me" (John 21:15–19).

Being Led by the Spirit

While the Spirit of God has been a recurrent presence in the whole story we have traced so far, from creation through the resurrection of Jesus, the book of Acts brings to the forefront the Spirit's agency and power in creating and leading a new community.

The gathering of Jews from disparate nations in Jerusalem for Pentecost becomes the occasion of a polyvocal testimony to God—many voices in different tongues and cultures expressing powerfully that God is doing a new thing. The gift of the Holy Spirit that comes upon the new believers knits them into patterns of communal life characterized by sharing, generosity, and praise (Acts 2:42–47). Their lives are broken open toward one another and toward the world.

When we read through the narrative of Acts, we find continual emphasis on the power of the Holy Spirit in giving the apostles words to testify to what God is doing. We find the Spirit leading them across cultural barriers as they experience persecution in Jerusalem. We find the Holy Spirit connecting people once divided by religion, culture, ethnicity, and religion. Healing, which involves the restoration of community, is a central feature of these stories.

And yet, so is conflict and confusion. We find in Acts 6 complaints among Greek-speaking members of the community because their widows are being neglected. We find bold followers like Stephen being martyred. We find Philip being led by the Spirit to accompany an Ethiopian court official on his journey as he seeks to make sense of Isaiah, but then being snatched away (Acts 8). We find Saul, a keen opponent of the Way of Jesus, blinded by an encounter with the risen Lord. Disoriented, he only recovers his vision after three days of fasting, when the disciple Ananias lays hands on him (Acts 9). We find Peter resisting the Spirit's call to eat with and baptize the household of a Roman army officer, Cornelius, only to have his understanding of the gospel provocatively expanded through this encounter (Acts 10).

The mission to the Gentiles under the Spirit's leadership brings conflict, as the early Christian community must renegotiate its understandings of cultural identity and purity (Acts 15). Paul and his coworkers do not always get along. There are imprisonments, torture, arrests, lots of travel, new churches being formed, riots, shipwrecks, debates, powerful testimony, evidence of the Spirit's work in signs and wonders, and ultimately martyrdom for many. It is a nomadic and residential adventure of being pushed into new experiences by the Spirit of God in order to show God's healing power to people where they are. It is a story embodied in the community of those who tell it, a community expanded and multiplied as new leaders emerge and new populations share in its promise. It is a journey of learning, new creation, changed imagination, trial, and failure. It is shaped by practices of prayer, discernment, storytelling, and witness in relationship. In some respects it is simple, but never easy.

Restoring Community in a Participatory Age

As we explored in chapter two, inherited structures and patterns of community are collapsing in today's world. Identity has become a fragile and fraught construct. The paradox of the twenty-first century is the simultaneous disintegration of traditional expressions of community and the rise of a participatory culture. Even as forms of association and belonging that once brought Americans together in previous generations have crumbled,[5] people are now loosely connected through social media into virtual communities that they cocreate. Ours is a world rent by divisions, in which technology splinters as well as unites us. It is a nomadic world of massive migration on the local, national, and particularly global levels. It is a world throbbing with the promise and failure of meaningful connection.

What does the Christian story have to say to a world of expressive individualism and self-authorship, of great beauty and deep injustice? To begin with, to be human is to belong. To be a person is to be in relationship—with our Creator, with one another, and with the wider created order.[6] The Christian confession of God is profoundly communal: God is not a solitary monad or isolated individual, but a relational community of persons, the Trinity. The very identities of the three persons of the Trinity are defined relationally with one another. The term "Father" (*abba*), which Jesus uses to refer to God, only makes sense as a term of belonging in relation to the Son. Likewise with "Son"—Jesus's identity is shaped by relationship with the Father, and both are united in the Spirit, whose identity is not a generic, abstract "spirit" but rather the Spirit of God, the Spirit of the Lord, the One whose presence and power breathe forth creation and lead Jesus in his ministry. To speak in a Christian way about God and personhood is to speak communally, to speak of a Triune God.

The classical theological word for this deeply relational and interpersonal conception of God's identity is *perichoresis*, a Greek word meaning "whirl," "rotation," or "circulation around the neighborhood."[7] In God's life, difference and otherness are the basis of unity, not the cause of division.[8] The divine community is a community of mutual sharing, exchange, indwelling, and interdependence not closed in on itself, but generative, creative, and outward-reaching. God creates the world for community.

The character of that community reflects the interdependence and mutual belonging of God. Humanity is created in the image of God for flourishing in a web of interconnectedness with God and the earth (Genesis 1:27–28). We are created as distinct from God, with our own human creaturely integrity, to rely upon our Creator and participate in God's creative care for the world. We are created distinct from each other, each person possessing uniqueness, to share life together. Difference and otherness are intrinsic to the design of creation.

It might be easy to hear these ideas about God, community, and personhood as beautiful abstractions far removed from the realities we face in a world of broken families, neighborhoods, and societies. But the Christian confession of God as triune, grounded in the biblical narrative we have explored above, insists the opposite. It is a confession that God meets us where we are—that God is in fact "circulating around the neighborhood," not just off somewhere in heaven. It confesses Jesus not merely as a wise teacher, prophet, or sage, but as "true God from true God," both sharing fully in the divine life and "born under Pontius Pilate," a victim of empire, torture, and violence.[9] It proclaims the Holy Spirit as a personal presence who makes God knowable to us in the here and now. It is a far cry from the God of Moralistic Therapeutic Deism. The Trinity is the Christian way of describing a God involved in human affairs, who transcends the world in ultimate mystery and yet also enters the world at the most particular and concrete, who is timeless and yet present, powerful, and active even today.

Throughout Christian history, people have been tempted to reduce this rich classical conception of God in various ways. The idea that God would take on flesh and move into the neighborhood and go as far as to suffer and die with humanity was even in Paul's day "a stumbling block to Jews and foolishness to Gentiles" (1 Corinthians 1:23). The early church battled heresies that saw Jesus as subordinate to God the Father or less than fully divine. There's something strange about God getting so mixed up in human life! It can seem easier to bracket God out from the world. Then we can go on our own to create our destiny, control things, write our own stories, and realize our own fates—the contemporary cultural story.

Yet if God is aloof, isolated, disconnected, bracketed out of daily life in the world, unwilling to reach us where we are, there is no hope. We can try all we want to pray and meditate fervently, work our hardest to establish justice and peace, do our best to manage human circumstances as efficiently as possible, but suffering, estrangement, violence, and death will always catch up with us in the end. We are caught in a matrix of mistrust, disobedience, fear, self-centeredness, lust, and greed from which we cannot free ourselves. Much as we try to build a perfect world (the modern Western technological dream), there is too much brokenness in us and in our relationships for this to work out. We cannot save ourselves.

The good news of God in Christ—developed so fully in the biblical narrative—is that we don't have to. God has saved us and is saving us by entering the neighborhood and joining us, in the thick of the human condition, in order to restore us to community with God and one another. This includes enduring abandonment, betrayal, suffering, rejection, torture, and death in the most shameful manner possible in Jesus's day. God meets us not only in the best and brightest of where we are, but the worst. When the Spirit raises Jesus from the dead, breaking the ultimate hold of death on humanity, we see tangibly an alternative future of healing and restoration in relationship with God and others. That future becomes our future, tasted in the present.

God's mission is about forming and restoring community. Humans are made for belonging and given freedom. Our tendency is to misuse that freedom to turn away from God and others. God's response to humanity's rejection of right relationship and trusting dependence on God is to call specific people and through them to form a community of promise—Israel. The calling of Israel is not a privilege, but a responsibility, as God works through the particular for the sake of the universal. When Israel's own communal life is distorted by injustice and oppression, God raises up prophets to call the people back to right relationships.

Jesus's ministry involves the building of community, a community that crosses divides of culture, religion, and gender in his setting. The community that Jesus leaves behind finds itself turned inside out by the power of the Spirit, from despair and fear to bold witness. The Spirit joins together unlike people from many nations and cultures into a new community called and sent to witness to God's reconciliation of the world in Christ. When we are "in Christ" (2 Corinthians 5:17) our identities are renewed and reborn. We live for God and one another, not just for ourselves; we belong to God and one another, no longer just to ourselves. The Spirit reorients our identities toward a new, shared community. This reorientation involves a decentering of the self, not a negation of individuality and uniqueness, but a restoration of self into right relationships of mutual belonging. The Bible's ultimate vision is one of community: a heavenly city where mercy and justice prevail and all the nations are healed (Revelation 21–22).

The Renewing of Our Minds

God's people have found themselves in circumstances of massive cultural change and upheaval before—circumstances that upended established patterns of religious life and community, moments like the wilderness and exile. The Christian story is a story of people being healed and restored to unity with one another, of life coming forth from death. In God we have an immeasurable worth that we can neither earn nor lose; we don't need to make it all up on our own, and we're not ultimately alone.

Now is the time to claim that identity as we learn what it means to "put on the mind of Christ" in a culture that views and experiences reality very differently. We are hardly the first generation of Christians to confront a culture that needs conversion by the gospel. If the primary challenges facing the church in its life and witness today are cultural, spiritual, and theological (not merely organizational, financial, institutional, or programmatic), we must attend carefully to what it might mean for us to "let the same mind be in you that was in Christ Jesus" (Philippians 2:5), or to be "transformed by the renewing of your minds" (Romans 12:2). How do God's people experience the transformation of their minds so as to see, interpret, and experience the world in light of the triune God's presence and activity? Such a process involves *learning* through the work and influence of the Holy Spirit. It unfolds experientially through practices and relationships with God and others. As we have seen in the biblical discussion above, it often involves mistakes and misunderstandings. It upends the status quo. It is not an easy road to follow. But the path Jesus calls us to and travels with us demands all of us. We are called to lose our lives in order to gain them (Matthew 16:25).

In the face of these cultural changes and challenges, there are simply no easy answers. In the culture that has emerged around (and within) us, there is much that runs contrary to the gospel. There is also tremendous opportunity to rehear the gospel, to deepen the church's identity and practice, and to learn how to form community with new neighbors. We need to rediscover how to be the church in a world after cultural establishment. While the cultural currents are complex, the ways the church must respond are actually rather simple, concrete, and accessible to ordinary disciples.

We need to find ways to inhabit and practice a different story than the predominant ones that the church has indwelt in recent times—stories shaped deeply by the cultures of establishment and secularism.[10] These stories tended to eclipse God's presence and agency from the world and church, leaving us in charge. Mission was something the church did *for* God, rather than something integral to God's ongoing life in which the church participates. In the establishment era of political, social, and cultural privilege, the church could use its power and resources from a place of relative invulnerability in its engagement with the neighborhood or others across the world. The church has often exercised mission as a benefactor to those less fortunate—dispensing charity from a position above those served, without having to risk deeper relationships of mutuality. (It is important to note that Jesus names the benefactor posture in Luke 22:24–27 explicitly and challenges his disciples to a different approach.)

In fact, research on social service mission efforts in American congregations finds them to be largely programmatic and episodic, undertaken by a small percentage of congregation members, with little opportunity to form relationships.[11] In seeking to attract new members, the church has also often sought to welcome neighbors into its established life on its cultural and social turf, rather than risk forming new expressions of Christian community on the neighbors' turf. As the body of Christ, however, we are sent to join up with people where they are, to listen deeply to their lives, and to discern together with those neighbors what new life God is bringing forth.

Our imaginations change through practices and experiences over time. There is no shortcut through the wilderness, only the daily disciplines of coming to trust in God's provision and following the pillars of cloud and fire step by step. There is no quick rescue from exile, only the practice of dwelling by the rivers of Babylon to sing the Lord's songs even amidst a foreign culture. It is through rehearing the Christian story and practicing the Christian life together, day by day, that we come to a new and more faithful way of seeing and experiencing the world.

Conversion and Translation

The mission scholar Andrew Walls argues that Christianity has two deep impulses—to be at home in culture, and to be in tension with culture.[12] For too long, the church in Western societies has been too much at home in culture. It has lost the turning, the change of mind, the renewal of imagination and life—the conversion (*metanoia*)—that is at the heart of the gospel. Walls points out that the incarnation is itself a kind of translation—divinity is translated into humanity in Christ as a prelude to repeated acts of translation of God's Word into all cultures through the body of Christ.

This work of conversion, which is the Spirit's work in, through, and beyond us, is the primary work facing the church in our society. It involves rehearing the gospel in its fullness, a gospel that calls into question the presuppositions of every culture even as it is expressed in that culture.[13] The gospel is always embedded in particular cultures—that is the logic of the incarnation. Our own rehearing of it invites us into the posture of being learners (disciples) who seek the Spirit's leading as we are called into God's great adventure of faith. That calling is always also a *sending* into relationship with our neighbors, for God creates covenant community not primarily for its own enjoyment or privilege, but to be a blessing to the world (Genesis 12).

In God's promise and call we find a new identity—an identity that frees us to be able to risk our very lives, because we have a secure future. God's promises of grace, unconditional love, the ultimate restoration of community, and eternal life free us to embrace a posture of trial, failure, and experimentation precisely because it isn't all up to us. We aren't in charge—in charge of our churches, in charge of Western culture, in charge of our neighborhoods. We don't know quite where we're going. We have a great deal to learn. God never promises that the path will be straight, direct, or easy. It indeed leads through the valley of the shadow of death, but as the psalmist says, we don't travel it alone.

In the next chapter, we'll look to glean wisdom from organizations that are discovering how to embrace agility. They are doing so by practicing deep listening to neighbors in order to engage real and complex problems. They are failing often and well and learning from those failures in order to connect meaningfully with others. These practices begin to flesh out how we might concretely reenvision our life together as learners of Jesus's Way in today's world.

Questions for
Discussion

1. Which biblical character(s) do you identify with most as you think about your own journey and calling?

2. If God meets us where we are in Christ, what might that mean for your church's relationship with its neighbors as the body of Christ?

3. Was there ever a time in your life when you came to see and interpret the world differently? How did that happen?

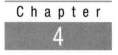
Failing Well, or What the Church Can Learn from Silicon Valley

Several years ago, our family's trusted vacuum cleaner finally died after many years of use. We did some research and decided to replace it with a Dyson vacuum. The Dyson vacuum is a remarkable thing—it uses a cyclone to generate tremendous power, drawing dirt out of our carpets we never knew was there. It is environmentally friendly because it doesn't require disposable bags.

The Dyson vacuum was the result of a lengthy process of learning, however. Over a five-year period, James Dyson made 5,127 prototypes before he got one to work right—over five thousand failures! For Dyson, the serial inventor behind the bagless vacuum, the ballbarrow (an ingenious wheelbarrow that tilts in any direction), the bladeless fan, and many other devices, this rate of failure is par for the course. He says, "It's when something fails that you learn. If it doesn't fail, you don't learn anything. You haven't made any progress. Everything I do is a mistake. It fails. For the past 42 years—I've had a life of it."[1] These are the words, by the way, of a billionaire who has been knighted for his accomplishments. What kind of posture of humility and resilience allows one to sustain so many failures in order to get to something that works and connects?

Failing Forward in the Face of Uncertainty

As we have been discussing, the realities facing the church today are complex and ambiguous, realities for which there are no quick and ready-made solutions. In our culture of technical expertise and professionalism, we look to leaders to resolve this ambiguity by providing quick fixes, giving us a clear map of where to go, or offering the program, project, or plan that will get us out of this wilderness back into what was comfortable and familiar. For many churches, that means trying to return to a time period in which the culture supported church participation and Christian identity. For others, it means replicating proven models of what church should look like, rather than engaging in the messy discernment of bringing forth something genuinely new.

The leadership scholars Ronald Heifetz and Marty Linsky distinguish between *technical problems*, for which the answers already exist and only need to be applied, and *adaptive challenges*, which require new learning on the part of the people facing them.[2] Since adaptive work is difficult, involves loss, and demands that we all share responsibility for the learning, our human tendency is to resist it. We would rather have experts fix things for us. But experts don't have fixes for the primary challenges facing the church today. We all need to shoulder the work of learning together. This learning is less about applying some proven principle or model from another context than it is about innovating our way into solutions through small experiments in a process of iteration, or repeated trial and failure.

The church has a great deal to learn about this iterative work from Silicon Valley, where organizations have developed the capacity to sustain massive levels of ongoing failure in the service of creativity, innovation, and growth. This is what thriving technology companies do every day. They inhabit a highly fluid industry that brutally punishes those who grow complacent or disconnected from their customers. These companies' culture and practices have much to teach the church about making good mistakes.

Agile Project Management

Years ago, software development proceeded through a sequential, linear process. The end product was clearly envisioned, and a careful plan with detailed steps was laid out in order to manage the way from the present into that future. Components of a program would be built by teams and then passed to the next team, who would add to them until the original vision was realized. Then it would be tested rigorously for bugs before being delivered to customers. This approach makes several key assumptions, which used to function reasonably well: we know what the end product will look like; we know how to get there; and we have the time to build it piece by piece in sequence. Everything was centrally controlled. The work was largely technical—applying existing expertise to finite problems.

In recent years, however, the marketplace has rendered this traditional approach increasingly problematic. In today's fluid environment, many customers don't know exactly what they need at the outset, and even if they do, those needs tend to change repeatedly along the way. While there are still major dimensions of the work that are technical in nature, there is also a lot of adaptive learning involved—innovating new solutions to complex challenges as we go. The destination isn't fully clear, but it emerges through shared ownership and vision among all those participating—both the customer and the developers. There are multiple points in the process at which adjustments and redirection are possible based on ongoing experimentation in close consultation with the audiences being served.

This new approach, known as agile project management, is increasingly becoming the norm.[3] It involves much greater attentiveness to what is going on outside the organization than the old approach. Workers are empowered to improvise and collaborate in new ways. The customer is actually a partner in discovering what the product should become, as end users are incorporated into the learning process. Various dimensions of the project are affected by new learnings that arise. Leaders are less responsible for controlling a predetermined process than fostering a lot of improvisation.

Lean Startups

One example of an agile approach is lean startup methodology. You're familiar no doubt with the archetypal story of a Silicon Valley startup company. A smart engineer has a brilliant idea and starts tinkering in a garage. She convinces venture capitalists to pour money into the project as a company is formed and the product built, which can often take years. When the idea is finally brought to fruition in the form of a completed, well-designed product, it is launched into the world with a big marketing splash in the hopes of finding customers. Sometimes this works really well. But more often it doesn't. This traditional approach to starting companies is very expensive (both in money, time, and energy) and risky, because the failures are so big.

A new approach has emerged that embraces countless small failures to avoid big expensive ones.[4] Lean startup methodology begins with ideas for a product or service that will connect with people in the marketplace. But those ideas are held lightly—as provisional rather than definitive approaches. The key to the lean startup approach is a tight ongoing relationship with audiences who help teach the company what its products need to become. This happens through building and testing quick prototypes and engaging in continuous listening loops. Rather than invest a lot of money in a finished product and hope it connects with where people are outside the organization, lean startups find users out there who will try out "minimum viable products"—experimental versions—at every step of the way. Sometimes these are alternatives tested with different groups simultaneously. The posture of the company is one of humility and learning as it expects new insights to come from users. Rather than getting overly invested in polishing *its* internal ideas of what to create, the lean startup approach embraces change and redirection based on what its audiences actually need.

This process of rapid prototyping (lots of small experiments, most of which will fail) in close conversation with audiences often leads to points of inflection, or *pivots*. These are moments at which the new company realizes that the path it had originally envisioned taking is not where it actually needs to go. In response to what people out there are saying, the company must pivot, or change direction. Because the whole process is lean in its use of resources, and the company hasn't overly committed to a single direction or outcome, pivoting is relatively easy. It will involve loss, but those losses are minimal compared to a traditional approach. Integral to this whole process is staying connected to outsiders, providing channels by which they can share feedback, and taking seriously what they say. It is about meeting them where they are and expecting to learn from them.

Design Thinking

I entered college thinking I was going to become an engineer. Enrolling in an introductory engineering class during my freshman year provided a very helpful failure for me. In the process of receiving my lowest grade ever, I realized I was called in a different direction academically. But I remember vividly one of the field trips we took in that class, down University Avenue in Palo Alto to the offices of IDEO. At the time, IDEO was a relatively small design firm populated by a quirky group of engineers, artists, and creative people, most with Stanford connections. The IDEO offices were open and whimsical, with all sorts of odd objects hanging from the ceiling and strewn about on tables. Dress was decidedly relaxed, and there were unfinished projects everywhere. It looked a bit like a playground for adults.

At the time, IDEO was on the path to becoming the world's leading design firm, responsible for countless innovations that people use every day, such as Apple's first mouse. They have pioneered an approach to solving problems called "design thinking" that holds some key lessons for the church.[5] Design thinking is about joining up with people where they are in the world, attending carefully to their ordinary lives, and improvising solutions to challenges they face. It applies to everything from making new consumer products (a better shopping cart or bicycle) to social entrepreneurship—addressing thorny social challenges such as increasing education for women in developing countries or providing safe drinking water.

Design thinking starts with a problem or challenge. These problems are often identified through close listening to people and inviting them to share what they are struggling with. The next step is the "deep dive"—intensive learning by observing people involved in the problem. From a design thinking perspective, it is not enough to *ask* people about their behavior, as people often don't recognize their own assumptions and patterns. One must *watch* how they live and what they do. Out of what is noticed in observation, collaborative teams engage in a process of rapid prototyping. These are quick and dirty solutions that take concrete physical form, not just beautiful concepts sketched on paper. Design thinking recognizes something very important—people learn through tangible experiences, not just ideas. The rapid prototypes are small experiments whose sole purpose is learning. Design thinkers realize that seeing, holding, tasting, and trying out things sparks the best insights. Failure is fully expected in these experiments—nothing is finished yet.

As these prototypes are tested, modified, and abandoned, solutions emerge. The assumption is that it will take many attempts (iterations) for a lasting result. One of IDEO's leaders, Tom Kelley, describes the attitude established early on at the firm: "You could stumble, as long as you fell forward."[6] IDEO recognizes that we live in a participatory culture, in which people seek experiences, not just ideas or products. People want to engage meaningfully, not just consume something.[7] Design thinking is a playful process of attending to people where they are in the world and embracing many small failures in order to improvise solutions.

Innovation and the Church

What are we learning so far from these organizations that know how to innovate?

1. *Innovation grows out of close listening relationships with neighbors.* It is not so much a matter of a solitary genius receiving a bolt of inspiration, as it is ordinary people joining up with other ordinary people where they are in daily life and attending to the realities they're facing. In individualistic Western culture, the myth of the solitary genius dies hard. But the best-known inventors, such as Thomas Edison, had whole workshops of people to collaborate with. Many great discoveries and inventions have happened just because people were paying closer attention to things that others ignored.

There is a genuine curiosity at play here that involves putting aside one's own agendas in order to take seriously other people's experience and expertise. Innovation is not about imposing one's own brilliant solutions on other people, so much as it is finding common ground with them in order to address real challenges they're facing. Even Steve Jobs, one of the brightest and most irascible innovators of the past generation, constantly drew on the synergy of teams of collaborators wrestling with the same questions and challenges. His brilliance lay in having such a strong sense of where ordinary people were—for instance, making computers far more user-friendly than they had been before.

Many religiously unaffiliated people in today's world don't have any sense that the church actually cares about their stories, hopes, struggles, and dreams. They instead experience the church as bringing answers to questions they aren't asking, trying to get them to join a religious club, judging and criticizing them—or most commonly, not even caring enough to have the conversation in the first place. The experimental Christian community Ikon in Belfast, Northern Ireland, once staged an interesting reversal of people's expectations around public evangelism. Church members went onto a public street and invited passersby to share *their* image or view of God on chalkboards or scraps of paper, rather than asking them to listen to the church's views. This experiment began to shift the conversation as neighbors disconnected from the church willingly shared their images and thoughts. In contexts in which the church has lost a lot of credibility, such acts of listening begin to build trust and the chance to engage in dialogue. Let me be clear: this is not to suggest that the church should simply accept and bless whatever people in the culture believe. Rather, faithful witness to the gospel must take place amidst relationships and listening, which is a reciprocal process. The church cannot expect people to listen to its teachings without first engaging people where they are.

2. *Innovation involves iterative small experiments.* The cycle of rapid prototyping—trying things out, adjusting, and trying again—is integral to discovery and change. Churches often assume that trying something once means they have to get it perfect. If they fail, the whole endeavor (new ministry initiative, worship service, program, etc.) often just quietly disappears, without seeking to learn what changes might be made in the next round. Often, there is no next round. Churches tend to have unrealistic expectations for success. Innovators make clear that you have to try things out again and again, while making small modifications and reflecting upon your failures, to see what works. That is the value of small experiments—trying to connect with neighbors in small ways in which meaningful relationships might emerge and being willing to persist and try again when doors close. As we have explored, the biblical story is full of these sorts of failures, through which God's people learn what it means to participate in God's mission.

3. *Innovation requires a high tolerance for failure.* As entrepreneur Terry Jones observes, innovation is not like the Olympics, where you train for a decade only to win or lose, but more like baseball, where losing 70 percent of the time is pretty good.[8] There is simply no other way to learn than trying things out knowing full well they may not work. This idea represents a huge cultural shift for churches accustomed to the posture of establishment. In the establishment mode, the church assumes itself to be in charge, to have the answers, and to be competent. The idea of listening and learning from neighbors through processes of trial and error is quite foreign. It requires levels of humility and courage lacking in many churches. We are accustomed to neighbors coming to us when they are seeking God, not to seeking them where they are to inquire about their views of God. There are many good reasons why failure is difficult to tolerate for many churches. Chapter five will explore further how to address those dynamics.

4. *Innovation is about improvisation.* The most innovative organizations know full well that the future that emerges may not be one they planned on. There is a playful openness to something new coming forth. It involves the anticipation of surprise and the willingness to pivot in response to new information. Attempting to control the process of innovation usually kills it. Innovation opens up an unpredictable future, not a carefully managed one. Surrendering control does not mean that innovation is passive; on the contrary, the more active and participatory the better. It is highly intentional, but also open-ended. This is, of course, the kind of journey into which God invites Abraham, Sarah, Jesus's disciples, and other people in the biblical story.

The Danger of Focusing Inward

These practices and habits may seem foreign to many churches today because those churches are primarily focused on their own internal life. Innovation scholar Chris Trimble offers a provocative metaphor for this. At one point in history, Polaroid was known as a highly innovative company. Its signature snapshots that didn't require darkroom development prefigured today's digital revolution of instant images. But Polaroid, like Kodak, has been marginalized in the world of digital photography. How did this happen? Trimble observes that Polaroid was too focused on its cameras. It loved its cameras more than its customers. He asks the church: *Do we love church life more than we love our neighbors?*[9]

Innovation is a solution to a problem, and yet the church seems unclear about what unmet need or problem it is trying to address. The church should begin with questions people are actually asking in today's world, like "Who am I? What is love? What is the meaning of life?" Trimble points out that many people are interested in God and what the church might offer, but they are intimidated about approaching the church's established life, which seems closed off to them. In order to connect with these neighbors, the church must begin where they are and engage their questions first.

One of the paradoxes of innovation, as Clayton Christensen observes, is that innovators who succeed are often the most vulnerable in the next generation to failure. For instance, computer disk drives were first invented in the 1950s by IBM. Over the next thirty years, as the technology improved and uses expanded, IBM and several other firms established themselves as the dominant forces in the industry, catering to higher-end users. They used their technical and managerial expertise and abundance of resources to continue to improve the technology. This success blinded them, however, to the possibilities of creating cheaper, simpler versions for use in other devices. When emerging firms who didn't share the established firms' assumptions entered the market with inexpensive disk drives, IBM and other leading producers were caught off guard and quickly lost their dominance.[10]

This is an example of a *disruptive innovation*, or when established firms fail because they are undercut by emerging competitors who meet customer needs by offering simpler and cheaper solutions. This often occurs when established firms listen too much to existing customers rather than potential new ones.[11] That is, these firms were so captive to the needs and demands of their present audience that they neglected to pay attention to other audiences and to notice changes taking place in the environment. The disruptive innovators, by contrast, were connected to emerging audiences and realities and operated with different assumptions that freed them to meet needs that the established firms didn't even recognize.

The church tends to operate like a classic established organization, with its own loyal (but shrinking) base of members, participants, and supporters. Most churches are consumed with meeting the needs of the people already in their midst—trying to offer worship, cradle-to-grave programming, pastoral care, etc. The language, patterns, habits, and culture of those churches are tailored to speak to those already present. Paradoxically, effective leadership and management of these established congregations in order to sustain their current life often blinds leaders to what is going on in the neighborhood.

Meanwhile, many populations and generations neglected by the church are seeking to meet their needs for spiritual meaning, connection, and community elsewhere. From Moralistic Therapeutic Deism, to self-help books, to yoga classes, to meditation groups, to a whole range of formal and informal means by which people "tinker" spiritually, these approaches do not require the same kind of commitment as joining an established church. They are cheaper, easier, and more suited to the fluid culture of contemporary Western societies. From the perspective of many who choose this option rather than church, church is too intimidating, too complicated, too culturally foreign, and too distant.

The pattern described by Christensen does not bode well for established churches if they persist in their internal self-orientation, for established organizations typically lose out to disruptive innovators. This is because disruptive innovation involves *downward mobility*—divesting oneself of the elaborate, often expensive ways of operating that characterize the status quo of established organizations. The way that church is organized and conducted in many established congregations is simply too disconnected from where people are in today's culture. Alternatives that meet people's pressing needs for meaning, identity, and community in simpler and more accessible ways will thrive, as is increasingly taking place.

This is not to suggest that the church should capitulate to contemporary culture by reducing its life and witness to something quick and easy for today's consumers. In fact, a large part of the problem is that the church *has* reduced the gospel to an anemic version of itself. The reality is that many churches are quite fuzzy about who Jesus is and what his Way entails. The main focus may be around inherited forms of worship, programs, committees, or activities that no longer clearly and coherently connect where people are in their daily lives to the Way of Jesus. How can the rich treasures of church traditions and practices be clarified, deepened, translated, and renewed so that they might make sense in today's contexts?

Christensen observes that the reaction of leaders in established organizations to the emergence of disruptive change is often to work harder and try to plan better or smarter. While this kind of approach may help to sustain existing patterns, it fails in the face of disruptive change, because it tends to deny evidence about the nature of the disruption.[12] In other words, simply performing established patterns of church life better without addressing the underlying cultural changes will not suffice.

What can established organizations do? Christensen's research echoes much of what we discovered above. The only way to engage disruptive change is to "fail early and inexpensively."[13] Useful knowledge about how to connect with new audiences will only be gleaned through "expeditions" of listening and learning among those audiences, "testing and probing, trial and error," by engaging real people in real time.[14] In this work, having a lot of resources can actually be an inhibitor, because limited resources force an organization to be nimble and efficient. Large, established organizations are tempted to fall back into big, complex solutions that miss where people are. They are often more resistant to learning.

Positive Deviance

This discussion might seem overwhelming to many churches that cherish their traditions and practices and feel deeply threatened by the changes taking place around them. It would be easy to feel like we have to start from scratch to innovate forms of Christian community and practice that will connect with our neighbors. Yet that is not actually the case, for the future is typically a lot closer to us than we realize. In fact, it is often already present in our midst. A whole school of thought called "positive deviance" has arisen in recent years to affirm this reality.

Positive deviance has three simple premises: 1) solutions to seemingly intractable problems already exist; 2) they have been discovered by members of the community itself; and 3) these innovators (individual positive deviants) have succeeded even though they share the same constraints as everyone else.[15] Positive deviance is a powerful way to understand innovation precisely because it is not about importing a magical solution from outside (which rarely works) or expecting leaders to create a new future *for* the people. It is about God's future emerging *among* God's ordinary people, which is the biblical pattern. Positive deviance is actually quite simple; it just requires careful attending to one another and to the world.

Positive deviance originally emerged out of confrontation with a big, complex, seemingly insurmountable problem: childhood malnutrition. In rural Vietnam the malnutrition rate for children had reached 65 percent by 1990. Typically, addressing this challenge would have involved governments or aid organizations importing massive amounts of resources—food and money—alongside experts with plans, projects, and techniques. But infusions of outside resources tend to turn local people into passive, dependent recipients. Moreover, the political situation at the time disallowed that. Instead, the nonprofit organization Save the Children sent a couple of workers into the country. Due to hostility from government officials facing an economic embargo by the United States at the time, they were given six months—hardly long enough to make an impact, it would seem.

The workers could only look within the local communities for solutions, and that is precisely what they did. They mobilized villagers to look in their own midst for children who were not malnourished—the positive deviants. And they found them. These families were living under the same circumstances as everyone else, but somehow their children managed to be healthier. So the workers invited local people to observe carefully how these positive deviant families went about their days. Fairly quickly, they identified simple practices that separated these families from the rest of the village—practices like including tiny shrimp or crabs from the rice paddies in children's meals, stricter hygiene, and more frequent mealtimes. These practices were then shared by the villagers with one another. Once adopted, the malnutrition rate in that village would drop precipitously.

This same approach has been used extensively now in many other contexts around the world to address other complex, thorny challenges. Notice in the positive deviance approach that the answers are already present amidst regular people. They don't need to be imported from outside in the forms of programs or models. They don't require infusions of resources, which most church systems can no longer sustain. They consist of simple practices that some people in every community have discovered. The work lies in helping community members identify, share, and learn from those practices.

In the congregation I serve, Janice[16] is a positive deviant with respect to sharing her faith publicly in daily life. While many congregation members struggle with how to witness faithfully with neighbors in a culture that privatizes and restricts religious belief, Janice has developed ways of doing so openly and compassionately. She is a Caribbean immigrant who works as an early child and family educator among some of Minneapolis's poorest families. Much of her work takes place in homeless shelters. Janice regularly prays silently for the families she works with, and some of those families, including Muslims, have come to recognize her spiritual depth and have asked her to pray *with* them publicly. She has found that these families in crisis seek her out to lead them in group prayer and conversations about faith. Over time, this has become an integral part of her ministry in the workplace.

It would be easy for our congregation members never to know about this side of Janice's life. We had to create intentional opportunities for her to share it. One Sunday, the lead pastor interviewed her during the sermon about how she experiences and shares her faith in God in her daily work. It opened up a public conversation about the complexities of naming God in a supposedly secular workplace. We've encouraged Janice to share her stories, struggles, and learnings in adult forums and other spaces where congregation members talk about how they practice the Christian faith in daily life. Janice is a peer mentor on these questions in ways that the clergy could never be.

In every church, there are some members who are learning and practicing the Way of Jesus with greater depth and maturity. There are some ordinary disciples who are entering the biblical story and learning to interpret their lives in light of it. There are some women, men, and children who are connected relationally to neighbors outside the church and have found ways to engage those neighbors in conversation about the meaning and purpose of life. There are people who recognize that God has placed them in particular circumstances each day—workplaces, homes, webs of connection and influence—in which they have the opportunity to share God's peace with others. There are those who have discovered ways to pray, to give sacrificially, to offer hospitality, to practice forgiveness and reconciliation, to seek justice and peace for all, to take a day off (Sabbath), to serve in Christ's name. Yet most congregations are not organized around the kind of peer learning that would allow other members of those faith communities to hear their stories and struggles and learn from them.

This kind of learning is adaptive learning—discovery that emerges from the grass roots. It is not a matter of experts bringing solutions from outside, devising big institutional goals that will supposedly catalyze action, or crafting detailed strategic plans by which we expect to manage our way across the gap between our present situation and an aspirational future. The church has been given the gift of the greatest vision in human history—the kingdom or reign of God as announced and embodied in Jesus. That is our guiding vision, and it must be articulated and interpreted constantly in the church's life. But God's kingdom or reign is not so much an aspirational vision that we try to manage our way into as it is a reality already present in our midst—"The kingdom of God has come near" (or "is at hand") (Mark 1:15). It is God's gift and work, not our own, and it comes to us where we are, in the very midst of our uncertainty, doubt, failure, and confusion. It is not a project or program that we construct or implement.

Discerning the Kingdom

How can the church embrace its identity as learners of the Way of Jesus more deeply, drawing on the wisdom of these innovation practices, and engaging the small experiments and failures through which a new future emerges? It is through behaving and practicing Jesus's Way in relationship with one another and our neighbors that we come to see differently, not the other way around. We often assume that if people just get the right ideas about God, transformation will occur. Yet the biblical narrative we explored in chapter three suggests a different pattern, in which people experience an encounter with God that leads them into a journey of practice and discovery through which a right understanding emerges much later, if at all. It is more about relationship, experience, trust, and action—all of which bring about a new way of seeing and interpreting life.

Discerning the presence of God's reign in the ordinary circumstances of our world is central to the renewal of imagination
(*metanoia*) to which Jesus calls us. Where are formation and restoration of community in patterns of justice and mercy taking place?
Where is healing occurring? Where are the stranger, the widow,
the orphan, the alien being received, protected, and empowered?
Where are the shamed and guilty receiving forgiveness and being
brought back into right relationships? Where are resources and
authority being shared so that all may be empowered to flourish in abundance? What are the glimpses and foretastes of God's
heavenly banquet, around which there is feasting for members of
every tribe and nation?

This work of discernment, or attending prayerfully and won-
dering about what God is up to in the here and now in the power
of the Spirit, is not easy for many church people today because it
has not been their primary focus. We've been more accustomed
to asking questions about what *we* want our church to be, what
our members want in terms of programming and institutional life,
or how we're going to sustain church the way we like it, than we
have been to interpreting what God is doing in our midst and in
the neighborhood. If we've talked about discernment at all, it has
often been something occasional or episodic, likely delegated to
the clergy, church board, or a special team or committee rather
than shared by all. But the learning and discovery that the church
must embrace in today's environment cannot be delegated to the
few; it must be something that all disciples participate in, for they
are God's primary missionaries.

Like any other practice of the Christian life, discernment
requires intentionality. It takes repeated attempts over time to
grow deeper into it, just as learning a musical instrument does.
There is no way forward without failure. Discernment involves
regular and deep engagement with Scripture, not as a source book
of answers to our problems, but as the story that reshapes our

way of seeing the world in light of a God active in human affairs. It requires prayer—the capacity to listen and attend to God and others. It means learning how to say no as much as yes. Biblically, it often includes the presence of strangers through whom God speaks to us.

As we have learned from the innovation literature explored above, transformational learning emerges from careful attention to ordinary life, from close listening to neighbors, and from lots of improvisational experiments. It is God's ordinary disciples who are best positioned to do this work. It cannot be done *for* them by someone else. It must be participatory, because at its heart, it is about a new way of seeing and living in the world. God's reign confronts us where we are in the circumstances of daily life, calling us to repent (turn around, see reality differently) and join up with God's ongoing movement of restoration and reconciliation in the world. It is for each of us personally at the most visceral and particular level, and because of that also universal—for everyone, in every time and place.

My friend and colleague Alan Roxburgh makes a provocative assertion that I'll call Roxburgh's Rule: *to the extent to which leaders do the primary work of change in congregations, there will be no change.* Change must be undertaken, guided, and led primarily by ordinary members. There are multiple reasons for this. The first is that in adaptive work, the learning and discovery must come from the people. Second, leaders are often fond of beautiful new ideas, ideas that can easily be disconnected from where ordinary people are in their daily lives and experience. Change is less about getting those ordinary members to embrace aspirational ideas from leaders than it is about those members participating firsthand in entering the Way of Jesus in its improvisational embodiment. In other words, preachers can preach all they want about how glorious God's kingdom is, but until church members experience and learn to interpret its coming firsthand in the ordinariness of their daily life, little life change will take place.

As we will explore more fully in the next chapter, this does not mean by any stretch that leaders are passive. Their job is to create what consultants Ron Heifetz and Marty Linsky refer to as a *holding environment*, a relational space in which the people can do the work of experimentation and discovery.[17] A holding environment is uncomfortable enough that people must face the adaptive work but safe enough that they can risk engaging that work. Leadership involves interpreting the adaptive challenges and cultivating the environments in which people can address them together.

Becoming Close to God

The local church that I serve part-time in St. Paul, Minnesota, has been on an adventurous journey of discernment over the past nine years that has tried to take seriously the biblical teaching that God's Spirit is present among God's ordinary people. St. Matthew's Episcopal Church is in many ways an ordinary established church—founded 125 years ago, now in a century-old building tucked away on a side street in a residential neighborhood. There are only five parking spaces. It would be easy to drive by and not even notice that this church exists. The church would not seem very promising by the standards of church growth experts. It is neither large, hip, trendy, nor particularly wealthy.

Yet the remarkable things God has been up to in this local church are rooted precisely in its ordinariness and the ordinariness of its members. I have witnessed a powerful renewal of imagination and practice over nearly a decade that has emerged primarily out of learning to live into the belief that God is entrusting God's promises and callings to unfinished, gifted, complicated, regular people. Let me share a few stories about them.

Robert is a lawyer who has spent decades "seeking the peace of the city" (Jeremiah 29:7) by working in various private and public capacities to create job and educational opportunities for low-income residents of Minneapolis. He works with government officials, community leaders, and corporations to develop innovative partnerships that break the cycle of poverty, oppression, and despair endemic to inner-city neighborhoods by opening up pathways to education and meaningful and well-paying jobs for young people. Walking the streets of those neighborhoods with Robert means entering a web of relationships formed over years with everyone from local business owners to street people. Robert has repeatedly turned down more lucrative positions in order to serve "the least of these" (Matthew 25:40).

Barbara is a retired saleswoman and homemaker who has been a devout churchgoer and volunteer for much of her life. Recently, she was being fitted for new glasses when she struck up a conversation with the optical technician. Barbara was explaining how she dreaded a long winter car trip that she was about to take. The technician asked how she was going to get through it. Barbara explained that she was going to pray. The technician paused, looked intently at her, and inquired, "Are you close to God?" Previously, Barbara would have demurred and said no, keeping her faith private. But this time, she risked speaking the truth publicly: "Yes." A deeper conversation ensued.

Alice is a professional cellist who discerned a calling a few years ago to offer her musical gifts to the dying by playing at the bedside of people in hospice. Leanne is a physician who finds time in her busy schedule to pray for her patients each day between appointments as she participates in God's work of healing people. These are but a few vignettes of God's ordinary disciples coming to claim their participation in God's mission, of regular people learning their place in the Way of Jesus. They are not programs, organized church activities, or projects. They take place in the neighborhood, in ordinary life. None of it is scripted by church leaders; it is all improvised by these disciples in the power of the Spirit in relationship with their neighbors.

One of the challenges for our congregation is that the culture has shaped its members to operate primarily within the framework of "ethical spirituality"—the predominant way of understanding spiritual practice in contemporary life as described in chapter two. Ethical spirituality is about doing the right thing—being nice and fair and serving others. Yet it doesn't necessarily connect clearly to Jesus (other than as a moral example to emulate) and God's active presence in the here and now. So inviting people into deeper engagement with Scripture through practices like Dwelling in the Word[18] (a participatory practice of Scripture study) or *lectio divina* has been central to our work together. We had to create spaces in which ordinary disciples can try on various spiritual practices and talk about them.

Together, we have tried to redefine church membership less as institutional belonging and more as participation in the Way of Jesus in daily life. However, as we did so, we realized that we could not assume our members knew what the Way of Jesus looked like. One of the assumptions inherited from the establishment era is that people know the shape of the Christian life. But many churches—including ours—hadn't necessarily been clear about it. This became evident to our congregation when the church held a series of focus group conversations over a six-month period. Our church has become accustomed to being asked questions, whether in small group interviews, surveys, or informal conversations. We ask questions because the leadership is trying deliberately to create space for people to share where they are—their questions, realities, challenges, hopes, and dreams. It is too easy for church leaders to assume they know what these are rather than actually finding out. Since I had recently published a book called *People of the Way* about renewing the church's identity in becoming learners of the Way of Jesus,[19] it made sense to inquire more deeply how our own members understood what that meant.

A small team was formed to lead this inquiry. By asking questions like, "What does it mean to you to follow Jesus in daily life?" they discovered that even after years of preaching and teaching about discipleship, members of our congregation were all over the place. They lacked a clear and coherent common understanding of following Jesus in the world. We realized the need to find ways to articulate the shape of the Christian life in language the people of our congregation could understand. A new round of listening in groups began as we tried together to find language that was indigenous to the local vernacular of this congregation—words that actually made sense to people.

The product of this process was a "Way of Life" that reads as follows:

> St. Matthew's Episcopal Church is a community of people invited by Christ to meet him at his table, in each other, and in our neighbors. As apprentices, we practice following the Way of Jesus as expressed in the Anglican tradition, in the power of the Spirit, so we can participate in God's healing of ourselves and the world. We understand Jesus's Way to embody these themes:
>
> - **Story:** Learning God's story and finding ourselves in it
> - **Prayer:** Attending with openness to God and the world
> - **Simplicity:** Decluttering our lives so we can be faithfully present to God and one another
> - **Discernment:** Reflecting together on what God is up to in our lives and neighborhood using Scripture, tradition, and reason
> - **Reconciliation:** Joining God's movement to heal and bring people into relationship across differences
> - **Hospitality:** Opening space in our hearts and lives to give and receive in relationship with neighbors and strangers in need

- **Generosity:** Trusting in God's abundance and sharing what God has entrusted to us

- **Gratitude:** Living lives of thanksgiving for everything God has given us, and breaking bread with others in this spirit.

This statement is provisional and iterative. It is likely that it will already have been revised by the time you are reading this book. As the congregation listens and learns more, we may find more adequate language. But it serves as a map for our members to use to navigate daily life. It focuses congregational life around helping our members practice Jesus's Way—a Way that is no longer so fuzzy, no longer merely "ethical spirituality," but something deeper and more connected to the depth and richness of Christian tradition and God's presence in the here and now. Each of these practices is now serving as a focus for conversation and Christian formation for all ages.

Such experiments in listening and reinterpreting are integral to the life of an agile church. At our congregation, they have taken many forms. We've used Appreciative Inquiry to identify our congregation's strengths through collaborative storytelling.[20] Several years ago, we engaged in a congregation-wide discernment process designed to surface themes and images that would help us interpret the future God was calling us into. The church board spent two meetings developing a question to ask the congregation and came up with the following: "When you consider the gifts we have been given and the needs of our world, what future do you imagine God is bringing forth in our midst?" That language is very intentional—it reflects the biblical and theological commitment that God is actively creating a new future, a future that is not just a distant aspiration, but actually already present in the ordinariness of daily life. This future is perceived imaginatively through the renewal of our vision in Christ. It is in our midst.

The difficulty with such a question is that it can seem pretty abstract. If you ask ordinary members to answer it, they will likely assume there is one correct answer that leaders already know and so will be afraid of being shamed if they don't get it right. So they will either be reluctant to answer at all, or will offer very pragmatic answers ("Let's renovate the kitchen!"). Or it might default into the idea that the church has gifts or resources simply to plug needs in the surrounding community, rather than to enter into deeper relationships of reciprocal sharing with neighbors.

We were blessed during this season in our church's life to have a leader on our staff who used playful, indirect means to invite the congregation into this question. He gathered groups from across the church, began with a simple practice of dwelling in a scriptural text (in which people are invited to share where their imaginations get caught), and then engaged the question creatively. For our hospitality ministry team, he asked them to develop a menu together that represented the future God was bringing forth. What dishes, from what cultures, would be on it? For the art ministry team, he asked them to paint or draw responses, and then to talk about them. He had groups of adults build answers to the question out of Legos and then interpret their creations. Parents of young children were asked to bring a children's book that suggested an answer to the question. All of these exercises were fun, engaging, and playful. They yielded rich images and themes that helped the congregation interpret what God was up to in its midst and where God was calling us to go.

One night, a man named Ben (not his real name) showed up at one of these sessions. He was experiencing homelessness and had been loosely connected to our congregation for several months, as a few of our members had taken him to medical appointments. Ben participated regularly in a weekday Bible study, where at his request, members of the church laid hands on and prayed for him. This was during the height of the Great Recession, and beds in homeless shelters for single men were nearly impossible to find in the Twin Cities. He had been sleeping some nights in our church. He came that night looking for Bible study and was encouraged to stay for the discernment conversation, especially as it began with dwelling in Scripture. As the question about the future was put forward, he sat up on the edge of his seat: "*I'm* the future God is bringing forth in your midst. Every other church treated me like a problem to be solved, but you treated me like a human being."

It is only by God's grace that a few of our congregation members had embraced Ben—there are a lot more vulnerable people in our neighborhood with whom we've failed to connect. But we realized that all those biblical stories of strangers bringing a blessing and calling, as they had to Abraham and Sarah, were coming alive in our midst. Ben was calling us into a deeper way of doing ministry with neighbors in our community—not through projects or programs, but through relationships.

Ben disappeared several weeks after that night, but he showed up again last summer, just as we were putting together the Way of Life statement above. He has housing now and a job helping other people experiencing homelessness. He was thrilled to share this good news with us. We believe Ben was sent by God in yet another moment of key discernment for our congregation to remind us who we are and what we're called to become. He was inviting us, like Abraham and Sarah, into the journey of God's mission.

How do God's ordinary people come to recognize and claim their callings in God's unfolding story? What are the disciplines of an agile, learning church? The next chapter will delve deeper into how congregational life can be reshaped around becoming learners of the Way of Jesus who embrace small experiments and learn from their failures for the sake of becoming close to God and connecting with neighbors.

Questions for
Discussion

1. As you consider the life of your church, where might the future be already present in your midst? Who might "positive deviants" be from whom you can learn together as a community how to practice the Way of Jesus more deeply?

2. What relationships with neighbors already exist in your congregation's life through which you might learn more about the surrounding community's hopes, struggles, and dreams?

3. What kinds of iterative small experiments might your congregation be called to that would help you connect more deeply with your neighbors?

Disciplines of
a Learning Church

or years, I've been involved in helping coach my son's soccer teams. As anyone who has coached youth sports knows, it is all about learning through trial and failure, practice, and most of all, *play*. No one likes mindless, repetitive drills. The best moments are when the players freely improvise within the constraints of a game. They have to try out a skill or pattern through embodied experimentation. The more playful the better, since play invites forth creativity, spontaneity, and freedom of spirit. The best learning takes place when there is laughter on the field.

Soccer offers a wonderful metaphor for innovation. It is a game with all sorts of structure—the boundaries of the field, rules, technical skills, time—but also a wide-open canvas for improvisation. The players have to make things up as they go in a fluid and collaborative way. When players don't communicate, freeze up, try to go it alone, or won't take risks, the game breaks down. The best teams play in a flow of extemporaneous movement that is the result of hours of practice and the fruit of many, many mistakes.

One of the reasons that American soccer teams have tended to lag behind their global peers is that in most of the world, the game is played from an early age on the streets, in parks, or in backyards largely informally. Kids spend hours trying moves out together, experimenting, failing, and teaching each other without any coaches around. The best American youth soccer coaches have learned to use their organized practice times to replicate this kind of free-flowing environment. When practices are overprogrammed and overdirected by coaches, the kids don't learn or grow as well. Good coaches instead offer structure, model the practices, and set players free to experiment and learn from their failures. A wise coaching mentor of mine taught me two excellent questions to ask after each game: "What went well today?" and "What would you do differently next time?" The players are invited to affirm the positive and also to articulate their learnings from mistakes, without being blamed or shamed.

Leadership in the agile church is about fostering the spaces in which people can learn, practice, and play. It involves creating the holding environment for adaptive work in which people can engage in relative safety with the tough questions for which there are no easy answers,[1] questions like, *How do we share our faith with younger generations who don't seem interested? How can we form meaningful community with our neighbors in the name of Jesus? How can we give witness to abundant life in Christ in a broken world? What is God up to in our neighborhood?* Rather than a quick and easy set of steps to follow, I want to invite you into a series of practices, disciplines, spaces, perspectives, and habits through which a new future might emerge.

Discipline 1: Cultivate Spaces for Conversation and Practice

The church must learn how to play if it is to embrace innovation. The posture of freedom, whimsy, spontaneity, and creativity that we inhabit when we play is vital for learning and growth. This idea represents a culture shift for many congregations whose formality and solemnity exclude playfulness, laughter, experimentation, and the open acknowledgment of mistakes. Whether intentionally or not, these churches communicate to participants a message that one must come to church buttoned up, polished, put together, and competent. The church presents itself before God as perfectly as it can be—through immaculately performed worship, entertaining programming, and flawless operations.

The problem is that this approach fails to meet people where they are. Whole aspects of their experience are bracketed out as unwelcome or (implicitly at least) shameful. It also bears little resemblance to the biblical narrative, with its hapless, adventuresome, doubting, laughing, impetuous characters. When Jesus tells his disciples, "Be perfect, as your Father in heaven is perfect" (Matthew 5:48) what he's really saying is "be whole, be complete, be fully grown up" (*teleiois* in Greek)—not "get everything right." The biblical story suggests that we only get to maturity through a lot of imperfection.

In the congregation I serve, we've discovered the importance of creating relatively safe spaces for people to practice and play in the Christian story and life. In fact, the most dramatic life change we've seen in our members has been through participation in peer learning spaces for conversation and experimentation. In a lot of churches, when the congregation gathers, it is often largely passive as clergy, musicians, teachers, and others "up front" perform prayer, worship, biblical interpretation, and other practices *for* them. This format may meet members' needs as spiritual consumers, but it doesn't foster learning and growth ("growing up" as in Matthew 5:48), because they never get much of a chance to practice prayer, worship, or biblical interpretation themselves.

For example, St. Matthew's in St. Paul has an adult forum on Sunday mornings that used to focus primarily on outside speakers offering interesting talks on interesting topics. While it was all quite interesting, we couldn't see much life transformation occurring through it. Over time, this space was changed into a peer-learning environment focused on practicing the Way of Jesus in daily life. It begins with Dwelling in the Word, in which people listen to Scripture together, sharing words or phrases that captured their imagination or questions that the text provoked in them. Sometimes, this sparks such rich conversation that it fills the whole hour.

Other times, we transition to discussion of a specific Christian practice, like hospitality or Sabbath, where with minimal framing from leaders, the participants are invited to talk about times in their lives when they've experienced or experimented with these practices. Often, there is a playful "homework" assignment of trying something out during the next week (like taking one day as a "screen Sabbath" and not using any electronic devices, or praying for a stranger). When we come back together the following Sunday, amnesty is declared for anyone who didn't get around to it, but those who did are invited to share what they learned. Congregation members teach each other how to live the Christian life, usually laugh together, sometimes cry together, and get to ask the real questions they're wrestling with each day.

A real shift in leadership for the clergy has occurred, because we were trained to be expert teachers who take charge and give answers. Doing so isn't very helpful in this case. It is better to be cultivators of a learning environment in which God's ordinary people bring their lives into engagement with the biblical story and Christian tradition.[2] Leaders can resource this conversation by framing it with texts, instructing people in practices, and sharing the richness of the tradition ("bringing forth treasures new and old"—Matthew 13:52). But they should not try to control it. Rather than bringing the leader's agenda, it involves trusting the Holy Spirit to work through God's people to shape the agenda collaboratively. While it might seem easier to fill the space and time with lots of information, it is more transformational to set the table for the Spirit to lead a conversation.

There are all sorts of ways in which people can be drawn playfully into this kind of engagement. We've used sticky note exercises where people are given notes to write what they feel are primary questions or challenges facing them. These are then posted around the room. Everyone has time to walk around and read the notes and to cluster them into themes that set the agenda for the conversation for the following weeks. We've tried out forms of prayer like the Ignatian Examen together as a means to reflect on how God is at work in our daily lives. We've used Dwelling in the World, a practice of reflecting back on the previous week and identifying a relational encounter in which you had an opportunity to share God's peace with someone. Participants are then invited to wonder about what God might have been up to in that encounter and what God might want to do if they were to reenter that relationship. They are then invited to share their experience with a partner.

There are endless ways in which spaces for conversation, experimentation, and discernment might unfold in different congregational contexts. For some churches, small groups are a primary means for this. For others, it is an adult forum or Sunday school class. It might be a neighborhood group or missional community. There is no single model or approach that will work everywhere—it is something to be experimented with. The key is cultivating a culture of participation and play in which people are not shamed for having the wrong answer, expressing a doubt or question, or failing. At our congregation, there are two couples attending the adult forum who don't come to worship yet, but they want to learn more about Christianity and engage questions with which they're wrestling. We have also been blessed recently by the arrival of a young woman who courageously asks questions that other people are probably thinking but hesitant to express. She usually prefaces her questions with, "I'm not sure if it is okay to ask this, but. . . ." We've gone out of our way to affirm that *yes*, those questions are welcome, and no one will shame her for voicing them.

Discipline 2: Address Fear and Shame

It is hard to overestimate the extent to which fear of shame blocks learning and innovation, particularly for adults, who naturally want nothing more than to avoid being exposed as incompetent. We live in a culture in which we are taught to evaluate our self-worth based on our perfection—our ability to perform, achieve, meet others' expectations, and generally keep it all together. Of course, underneath this for most of us are deep feelings of inadequacy and self-doubt. Researcher Brené Brown defines shame as the feeling that we are flawed and therefore unworthy of love and belonging.[3] Shame is the fear of disconnection, the breaking of relationships when people learn that we are not the perfect people we present ourselves to be. In this mode, vulnerability and weakness are things to be hidden at all costs.

Living in such a posture renders the kind of experimentation, failure, and playfulness we've been exploring in this book practically impossible. There is no innovation and learning without vulnerability. It is crucial for congregations to talk openly about these feelings and set them in the context of the biblical story, which repeatedly insists that human failure, weakness, and vulnerability are not grounds for God forsaking us. There is a crucial theological question at stake here—does God love me in all my imperfection, or is my relationship with God based upon getting it all right? I suspect many people in congregations today, even if they know that the first answer is what their churches formally teach, live haunted by doubt that the latter is really true. They feel they have failed God and thus are themselves deeply shameful—worthy not of love but rejection.

How can we communicate the extravagance of God's love? How can we invite people into the stories of the long-suffering, patient, maternal God of the prophets who binds Godself to God's people even as they reject God and God's ways? How can we help people experience the unconditional permanence of God's love and forgiveness in Christ that is *for them* personally? Without the capacity to imagine ourselves as chosen and called by God even and especially amidst our weakness, failures, doubts, and vulnerabilities, it is hard to comprehend how we can risk ourselves as learners for the sake of the gospel.

The key to getting beyond the paralysis of shame is to acknowledge it, to practice self-compassion that is rooted in God's compassion for us, and to trust that others will stay in relationship with us even when we are open about our faults and failures. Brown calls this living "wholeheartedly"—cultivating the courage, compassion, and connection that free us to embrace abundance rather than scarcity and so live creatively in the face of uncertainty.[4] From a Christian perspective, it means claiming the truth that we have been given worth by God that we can neither earn nor lose. This truth, which we must know personally, frees us to stay connected to God and others even as we make mistakes, for our ultimate value is not on the line.

The conversation in a lot of congregations must change so that doubts, mistakes, failures, and vulnerabilities are more openly acknowledged. Leaders need to model this. When leaders show up with their whole selves and stories, they give permission for others to do so, and the culture begins to change. People realize that they are not alone in their struggles. God's people have been here before. God meets us where we are. Grace becomes a reality felt and practiced by God's people, not just a beautiful idea distant from the mess in which we spend our daily lives.

Discipline 3: Engage Ambivalence and Conflict

The organizational scholar Chris Argyris explains that people in organizations tend to operate with defensive routines that are overprotective and inhibit learning. These routines include covering up mistakes, fostering secrecy, and avoiding embarrassment at all costs.[5] Our tendency is often to bypass problems, ignore inner contradictions, and cling to "espoused theories" rather than confront our "theories-in-use"—that is, the actual assumptions and values by which we operate in real life. An example of this would be a church that boldly proclaims "All are welcome!" on its website, sign, and bulletin, yet in its actual practice, shuts out any newcomer. Being welcoming may be the congregation's espoused theory, but the theory-in-use may in fact be preserving a warm and friendly environment for those who are part of the tightly knit extended family that is the congregation. There may be valid reasons to preserve that intimate community feel, but they are typically not named and examined. Then the church wonders why it can't retain any newcomers and feels shame about its failure to do so.

The way to break out of this kind of futile cycle is to engage in what Argyris calls "double-loop learning." This concept involves conversations that get beyond "What should we do?" to the deeper level of "Why are we doing what we're doing?" It means making values and operating assumptions explicit.[6] Double-loop learning involves asking simple questions that get at the assumptions that shape our behaviors. For example, a church might be frustrated that it is failing to attract unchurched people to a new "seeker-friendly" service that it is offering. But has it ever tested the assumption that unchurched people are looking for such a service? How valid is that assumption? It may have never been examined in actual conversations with unchurched people in the neighborhood. The more common single-loop learning is acting without getting to this deeper level of reflection.

Robert Kegan and Lisa Lahey remind us that there are often "competing commitments" that block people and organizations from learning and changing.[7] These are underlying values, beliefs, and behaviors that oppose the new, sometimes for good reason. For instance, a church might wish to be more flexible and innovative, yet it has deep competing commitments around avoiding loss and discomfort for its members. Or it may have a commitment to preserving a particular cultural legacy in worship and music that competes with translating its liturgical life into new cultural vernaculars spoken by its neighbors. These are legitimate commitments that must be addressed if any change is to take place.

Competing commitments are addressed by creating spaces of communal interpretation, listening, and discernment in which assumptions and values are surfaced and dilemmas engaged openly. People will only enter into conversation at this level if they feel that there is enough psychological safety, that their deeply held values and commitments will be respected, and that they will not be shamed. This work involves opening up and airing conflict in a learning environment in which people can negotiate real differences with one another or between their aspirations and underlying realities. There are good reasons why many congregations avoid this kind of work. It is demanding. Yet there is no way to lasting transformation without it.

This is what a holding environment provides—a container in which a community can name and wrestle together with its most challenging questions without being overwhelmed by anxiety, shutting down, or disintegrating. Shared norms, structure, and habits are required that provide the security for people to hang in there even as the discomfort rises. For churches, this may mean keeping simple practices of prayer, biblical engagement, or shared hospitality at the forefront to establish common ground. These may be long-established practices that everyone is familiar with or newer practices to which people can grow accustomed. Such structures allow the freedom to enter into difficult conversations and experiments together.

Discipline 4: Interpret the Present in Light of the Past

Leaders create holding environments for innovation in part by helping the community interpret its legacy, present situation, and future. This centers on asking questions to which leaders genuinely do not know the answer, questions for which there are no easy answers, questions that the community must own and engage. Organizational scholar Edgar Schein calls this "humble inquiry"—the art of drawing people out, building relationships based on curiosity and interest, and recognizing that we need each other's expertise in order to move into the future. Schein notes that status complicates the practice of humble inquiry in achievement-oriented cultures where knowledge and its display are prized, because such humility can imply a loss of status.[8] This is the case in many churches, where clergy are expected to tell more than to ask and already feel vulnerable amidst the huge challenges facing the church. Humble inquiry can seem to threaten their sense of identity, power, and position. Yet the community needs them to take this posture if innovation and learning are to occur.

Church leaders are curators and stewards of the stories and practices of the community, which means they must help the church identify a useable past. Again and again in the biblical story, leaders help people connect their present situation with God's faithfulness and promises. In the Hebrew Bible, the simple formulation "the God of Abraham, Isaac, and Jacob" evoked stories of God's blessing, call, and accompaniment of ancestors through difficult circumstances. The prophets tell and retell the story of God's steadfast loving kindness, often in relation to an ambiguous present. Jesus situates his own ministry within this rich history, reading from Isaiah 61 in his hometown synagogue and evoking a powerful message of liberation and redemption. Peter, Paul, and the early apostles preach about Jesus by retelling Israel's own story.

Where does a useable past lie in your church's history? I once had an opportunity to speak with a large group of Lutheran pastors in a rural Midwestern area where the population has been draining away for years as farms become larger and more mechanized. Their towns and churches are in decline. Moreover, the new neighbors who have arrived speak Spanish, Hmong, or other unfamiliar languages to these descendants of nineteenth-century Norwegian, Swedish, and German immigrants. Amidst the deterioration of a treasured and established way of life, it would be easy to succumb to despair.

But deep in their heritage is a pioneering legacy—the legacy of resilient nomads who came to this land seeking opportunity and started new churches under difficult circumstances. What might it mean for them to be pioneers today in a culture that no longer supports Christian practice? If their identity is in part being a church of immigrants, can they become churches for their new immigrant neighbors? One leader found an old sign in the basement of his church that read, "Norwegian service upstairs, English service downstairs." He hung this sign back up as a way of inviting his congregation into a different imagination about its identity. It changed the conversation about holding a Spanish service in this church, because people began to link their new reality with a bilingual landscape they had inhabited before.

This work of reframing the story in which people experience their world is vital for innovation, learning, and change. Scott Cormode explains that everyone operates with expectations that shape what they see. Culture provides a repertoire of meanings that we use to make sense out of a situation facing us. What Jesus did was to change people's expectations so that they could see, interpret, and experience the world differently.[9] In today's secularized culture, many church members operate with secular expectations and cultural meanings as they make sense out of their lives. This leads to profound reductions of Christianity like Moralistic Therapeutic Deism or ethical spirituality in which people interpret their experience out of contemporary secular culture's largely impoverished resources.

The renewal of mind that the gospel invites us to involves drawing from a different repertoire of cultural resources that can be woven into a narrative structure and lead to action. It means inhabiting a story in which our identities are a gift, not a project of our own construction, a story in which the liberating God of the Bible is up to something in our midst today, a story in which the Spirit of God is continually bringing forth new life, even out of death. It draws us deeper into the tradition and its rich stories and practices, deeper into our histories, and deeper into relationship with our neighbors in a posture of humble inquiry.

Discipline 5: Discover Open Spaces

What are the spaces in which learning conversations with neighbors can take place? The primary answer to this is the ordinary neighborhood environments in which church members relate with those outside the church—cafes, workplaces, backyards, playgrounds, schools, or other areas accessible to both church members and their neighbors. Many churches still assume that non-Christian neighbors must meet them on the church's turf, within organized activities sponsored by the church. Yet this simply will not work for many neighbors who find the church's programs and activities (including worship) intimidating, inhospitable, or irrelevant. The church has enough of a reputation in American culture for trying to manipulate people into belonging to it that many outsiders are quite skeptical, even if the church program or event ostensibly has a different purpose.

The American church might learn from some congregations in South Korea who are connecting deeply with their neighbors. These churches in the capital Seoul have discovered the power of "open spaces" for linking up with neighbors.[10] Open spaces are public environments for community life and gathering that are recognized by the neighborhood to be shared and accessible to them. These may take a variety of forms—a community center that hosts neighborhood groups, for instance, or a cafe. Even when they are owned and operated by a church, they are relatively neutral spaces for relationship-building and community life. More often, they are owned or hosted by nonchurch members.

A good place to begin in exploring open spaces is to find out where people already gather in your church's neighborhood, however you define it. Is there a café, community center, park, public square, restaurant, nightclub, fitness club, sports league, or other space where people naturally connect? One of the most powerful spaces I've had for forming relationships with neighbors is on the sidelines of my son's soccer games. In the suburban community in which I live, it is a good environment in which to get to know other families, hear their stories, and learn about their lives. It has been the setting for some of the deepest spiritual conversations with people of other faiths that I've had in recent years.

Such open spaces are vital because they become the grounds on which church members can get to know neighbors whom they might otherwise never meet. In the midst of sharing life (eating, playing sports, doing a service project, homework, or hobbies together), they cultivate the community that allows for greater listening and learning. The purpose of open spaces is not primarily to transition neighbors into church activities, programs, and membership. It is to form community, to serve neighborhood needs, and to learn.

One example of an open space ministry is the Front Porch in Austin, Texas,[11] which convenes public conversations about pressing civic questions like homelessness, poverty, and human trafficking designed not primarily for church members, but for the broader neighborhood. People from a variety of faith perspectives and no faith participate in these dialogues, which they call "The Elephant in the Room." The Front Porch also hosts worship in a pub, as well as concerts that include storytelling and conversation. While connected to All Saints Episcopal, an established church, the Front Porch functions as a different kind of public space in which to share conversation and community with neighbors.

The church must be very attentive to the power dynamics that come into play when neighbors are invited into its space, its turf, and its established life. One of the things our church in St. Paul has heard from neighbors we've talked to is that they wish the church could be more like the local public library, which is recognized as a common space for all. Relying upon the hospitality of neighbors in *their* spaces or otherwise neutral community spaces changes the shape of the encounter. Like the seventy disciples sent out by Jesus in Luke 10:1–12 to enter into surrounding towns and villages, carrying no money or baggage, the church must learn to depend upon the goodwill of neighbors as it finds ways in which to share God's peace with them.

Discipline 6: Be Present

The congregation I serve was integrally involved over a decade ago in transforming a former Episcopal hospital building in downtown Minneapolis into apartments for teenagers experiencing homelessness. Members of the congregation raised money and coordinated with civic leaders, other churches, and community partners to get the project done. When the formerly unhoused youth moved in, some of these same church members would go and talk with them and inquire about their needs. Did they need career counseling? Tutoring? Budget counseling as they were trying to get on their feet? To the surprise of these church members, the youth answered: *spiritual counseling.* They had access to all the other things through social service providers, but no one was accompanying them spiritually.

It took the congregation some years to discern how to respond to this call. Our church is not located in close geographical proximity to the apartments. Our own members weren't quite sure how to meet this need without just inviting them to church. They knew that proselytizing was inappropriate and would likely get them excluded from access to the building. Over time, however, the Spirit stirred in the hearts and imaginations of a few of our members who decided to launch a ministry of learning, listening, and presence with these youth.

Through relationships with a local social service center for youth experiencing homelessness, a few church members committed to simply showing up there and being available to talk or pray with the youth. The first few weeks, it didn't go very well. The youth and even staff were pretty skeptical about these unknown church members hanging out in the service center. But the church members persisted in showing up, even when no one talked to them. Eventually, their continued presence was noticed. Trust began to be formed, and conversations ensued. For these disciples who risked entering into a space not their own, incredible encounters began to unfold in which heartbreaking stories of suffering and hope were told and prayers shared.

The church members who were carrying out this ministry brought back regular reports. One of them, currently a seminarian, arranged to do her Clinical Pastoral Education (a kind of ministry internship) there. Stories of young lives broken by family abuse, addiction, and trauma, along with the incredible resilience of these youth, made their way into our congregation's life. For a congregation that has been housing homeless families in our building every August for over a decade and had received a calling toward deeper relationships with our neighbors experiencing homelessness from Ben, the man whose story I shared in the last chapter, it was clear the Spirit was up to something.

This endeavor has not, however, been without failures. For instance, we learned one year that many of these teens had nowhere to go for Thanksgiving dinner. Since our church hosts a free Thanksgiving meal that draws a wide mixture of people (church members and also neighbors and other guests), the leaders involved in the ministry with youth experiencing homelessness invited them to come. A number of the youth indicated that they were interested. Vans were arranged for rides to the church and church members were prepared to offer hospitality. But when the day arrived, none of the youth showed up. Even though they had relationships with some of our members and we had done everything we thought necessary to get them to church for the meal and welcome them, we underestimated the cultural barriers involved. Given their family backgrounds, many of these youth had likely never experienced a traditional Thanksgiving meal. Participating would make all sorts of demands on them, especially at a church with lots of unfamiliar people. This small failure, one of many, pushed us to learn more about the realities facing these neighbors.

I am not sure what God wants to do through this ministry, how long it will last, or what we will learn from it in the end. I do know that it is connected to how God has been active in our congregation's life in the past. It is grounded in relationships and callings that we have had for years. It will likely not result in many youth experiencing homelessness becoming members of our church. That isn't the point. The point is participating in God's reconciliation of the world in Christ, as people called to share God's peace and seek the flourishing of the city (Jeremiah 29:7). In that light, this experiment is priceless. It has drawn us into closer relationship with neighbors on their turf.

The power of being present over time should not be underestimated in the process of experimenting and forming community with neighbors. It simply takes time to build relational credibility; there is no shortcut around this. Sometimes this just means showing up, again and again. Jesus makes clear in Luke 10 when he sends the seventy disciples out that not all neighbors will be welcoming. But when the peace offered by those disciples is refused, it is not lost; it returns to them. One of the key learnings from Luke 10 for the church today is Jesus's injunction not to move about from house to house. Instead, he tells them to stay put and eat what is set before them—in other words, get to know deeply the realities facing these neighbors, to hear their stories, struggles, and dreams.

Discipline 7: Practice Your Way Forward

Being present over time is not only vital for cultivating community with our neighbors. It is also necessary for practicing and deepening faith. Innovation and learning for the sake of mission seem intimidating and overwhelming to many churches because they don't know where to begin. As we have been exploring in this book, we must begin where people are, for that is how God comes to us in Christ. This means creating spaces open to the questions people are carrying around inside them (whether our own church members or neighbors). Simple practices of listening to Scripture, learning to pray and attend to God, and interpreting God's movement in our daily lives begin to provide a grammar, a framework within which our imaginations are renewed.

Just like learning a musical instrument or a language, these simple practices must be tried again and again. The very structure and pattern of regularized habits is what frees us to grow and learn. I remember taking piano lessons as a child—it was not an instrument for which I was particularly gifted. Like many students, I wanted to jump ahead to play the songs I liked. I didn't want to practice the songs my teachers assigned, let alone do the scales that would build the agility of my fingers. Our family piano had an egg timer set on it that marked off the time within which I would practice each day. Much as I resented that timer (and was tempted to secretly adjust it ahead to get done more quickly), it created the space necessary for me to learn and grow. There is no learning and growth without the discipline of practice.

The kinds of practices that lead to growth and learning must be accessible to people where they are, like my piano teacher prescribing songs and scales that were neither too easy nor too difficult for me. They must be regularized and habitual, something we return to regardless of how we feel in a particular moment. They must build over time. There are always days in which practices go well and those in which they don't. There are moments of connection and moments of disconnection, times in which things flow together and others in which they seem to fall apart. Unless we keep at it, we never reap the benefits. This is countercultural in a society that focuses on instant gratification and experiential satisfaction, and that is all the more reason to invite congregation members into living as apprentices practicing the Way of Jesus together.

Discipline 8: Translate

Throughout this book, we've been talking about translation. The incarnation represents the translation of the divine Word into human life in the neighborhood so that God's life-giving gospel may be expressed in every culture through the body of Christ. The explosion in growth and vitality in world Christianity in the past half century coincided with independence from Western colonialism as the gospel and the church's life began to be more freely expressed in indigenous cultures and languages.[12] Throughout Western societies today, countless experiments are underway in translating Christianity into the culture of postmodernity to speak to new generations. These new forms of Christian community often very intentionally claim practices and rituals from the past, including ancient and medieval patterns that were dormant in their traditions for generations. Yet church life in these communities is framed within a postmodern cultural vernacular that emphasizes participation, informality, paradox, authenticity, and fluidity.[13]

The translation of the church's traditions and witness into different cultural vernaculars often requires an extended process of experimentation and innovation. The congregation I serve recently embarked on such a process with regard to a hallmark expression of its identity: worship. The congregation's proximity to a number of college campuses and a seminary has brought young adults regularly over the years. For some of them, typically those who grew up in our denomination, the traditional worship held on Sunday mornings speaks meaningfully. For others, however, it represents a cultural dislocation. They have yearned for ways of worship that were rooted in Anglican wisdom and practice but were also more accessible to them and their friends. A number of older members shared this yearning.

So a team comprised of those desiring alternative worship and those craving traditional expressions was formed to discern and experiment with a new service. This team met for many months while they studied the tradition, talked about their experiences, and reflected on the cultures present in the congregation and neighborhood. Then they began a series of trial services, to which they invited the congregation on Sunday afternoons. These services were clearly framed as experiments. Time was dedicated after each one for discussion and learning. Each of these trial services included lots of failure—some of the things we tried weren't faithful to who we were or accessible to participants.

Eventually, a new Sunday night dinner and service were started, largely led by young adults. It combines some traditional elements of Anglican worship (such as a simple order for Eucharist and written prayers) with fresh language, a more relaxed vibe, and a wider range of musical styles than Sunday morning. Since the official launch, it has been modified in many small ways as we have continued to learn.

The key to the process was bringing people deeply invested in the traditional legacy together with those newer to it so that they could learn from one another as peers. The work of study, prayer, and experimentation took time—lots of time. The congregation was invited into the experimentation in ways that did not disrupt their own normal participation in the Sunday morning service, but gave them freedom to offer constructive feedback. What emerged was not so much the realization of a leader's agenda or vision as it was a grassroots innovation that had been tested in the community and continues to be adapted as time goes on.

This is but one example of how innovation can unfold through the practice of translating the church's life and witness into new cultural vernaculars. It is crucial that in this work, newer members of the community or those from cultures other than the dominant culture (including youth) be empowered and given voice to shape what emerges. It must be a partnership, an accompaniment in which new interpretations of old songs can break forth while the community supports and encourages them.

Discipline 9: Improvise

The great twentieth-century organizational guru Peter Drucker once described leadership as conducting a classical orchestra—rehearsing until each instrumentalist was able to actualize the beautiful vision in the conductor's head for how the music should sound.[14] This is the kind of leadership for which many church leaders today were trained. They want to align everyone into executing the beautiful visions for ministry that they hold. Great conductors empower and free their orchestras to collaborate in fresh ways in order to bring alive a score that may have been inherited from many generations back. Every performance of a symphony is a unique and unrepeatable thing. But the score is clear, the path laid out, and the conductor in charge.

The jazz musician and organizational scholar Frank Barrett suggests that this model for understanding leadership and organizational life doesn't serve us well in the twenty-first century.[15] Jazz offers a better metaphor. Jazz is less about executing a predetermined script than it is about improvisation, whose Latin root *improvisus* means "not seen ahead of time." Jazz is about learning while doing, embracing imperfection, trying things out, and pushing boundaries—but all within shared structures and patterns. It is about collaboration and accompaniment, freedom and innovation.

Jazz is built on shared expectations and commonalities: the basic structure of a melody, rhythm, or song. These minimal structures provide the groundwork for improvisation. Jazz is fundamentally social, a collaborative effort among several musicians, and in so doing it creates space for a certain amount of autonomy and self-expression. Jazz only works when the musicians engage in "generous listening"—"an unselfish openness to what the other is offering and a willingness to help others be as brilliant as possible."[16] Accompanying, or "comping" for short in the language of jazz, is about sharing together in an emerging future:

> Organizational members have to make room for one another, suspend efforts to manipulate and control outcomes, relinquish investment in predetermined plans, and often surrender familiar protocols. To agree to comp, in other words, is to accept an invitation of openness and wonderment to what unfolds.[17]

This happens in part through the cycle of shared solos, where each member of a jazz ensemble takes turns improvising on themes while supported by the others.

Such improvisation often breaks expectations through pushing boundaries and making mistakes. Miles Davis once said, "If you are not making a mistake, it is a mistake."[18] Barrett urges dual aesthetics of imperfection and forgiveness that are grounded in an underlying confidence in the group. Control simply doesn't work in jazz. Jazz is about acting and paying attention to what unfolds, while being willing to "court disaster" by surrendering to the music and its possibilities, even as this takes the players to places that disrupt expectations.[19] This requires trust in one another and in the music that is emerging.

The church must trust that the Spirit of God is indeed alive and working among God's ordinary people as something new is brought forth in, through, and among them. The metaphor of jazz is instructive as an alternative imaginative space for churches to inhabit in ministry. When we identify the inherited practices and stories that order and shape our identity as people of the Way of Jesus, we are free to improvise upon them in new ways. These practices and stories are always culturally particular and embodied. Yet we sometimes confuse the specific embodiment with the story or practice itself, locking us into repeating an expression of church life that may no longer speak clearly to us or to our neighbors.

This is where the kind of double-loop learning referenced above comes into play. When we inquire of our practices, habits, and rules, "Why do we do this? What does it have to do with the gospel of Jesus?" we enter into deeper discernment about their meaning. Sometimes, that meaning is deeply buried, so obscured as to be lost. Then we need to break open the practices and habits and embody them anew. Like a jazz performance of a classic standard, there is considerable freedom to reinterpret the traditional tune, often playfully and spontaneously, to take it in new directions and to suspend expectations for the sake of birthing a genuinely vital and passionate voice.

Doing all this requires knowing the song and its traditions, of course. The work of discerning the cultural embodiment of the Christian life in today's contexts pushes us deeper into inquiring about the roots of things: Where did this particular expression come from? What is meaningful about it? How is it life-giving? These questions must be asked in a widely participatory way in a posture of humble inquiry. It is tempting sometimes to dismiss the relevance of habits and traditions without bothering to recognize first whether there are treasures in them. But every jazz artist knows that performing well in a group depends on drawing on common roots and riffs.

A tree can only be as fruitful as it is deeply rooted. Jesus uses this metaphor as he talks about the vine and branches: "Abide in me as I abide in you. Just as the branch cannot bear fruit by itself unless it abides in the vine, neither can you unless you abide in me" (John 15:4). We face a moment of significant pruning across the church, in which branches that are not bearing fruit are withering and being pared away. The key to flourishing, as Jesus indicates, is to abide in him and God's love.

For those who would understand the practices of innovation and learning described in this book as a layer of further activity to add on top of everything already being done in busy churches, that is missing the point. The work before us is about focusing and rerooting—discerning what to hold onto and what to let go of as we claim more deeply our identity in the gospel. It is about attending to God's presence and love, receiving God's promise for us, and abiding or dwelling. The actions that we are called to enter into must be rooted in God's life through the Spirit. Sometimes this means suspending activities and doing very little for a period of time in order to listen more deeply. Sometimes it means practicing Sabbath to remember that God is in charge.

The practice of innovating within established congregations brings with it all sorts of opportunities and challenges. Starting new forms of Christian community can allow for greater freedom of cultural reinterpretation. What does leadership mean within both of these, and how can church life be structured and patterned to foster innovation? These are the questions we'll take up in chapter six.

Questions for
Discussion

1. Where might a useable past lie in your congregation's life and history?

2. What fears keep your church from engaging in the tough conversations and risky experiments that might open up a new future?

3. What might it mean to translate cherished traditions and practices in your church into new vernaculars to speak with your neighbors?

Organizing for Innovation

y the late 1960s, Xerox had established itself as a dominant force in the copier and office-machine industry. Profits were flowing abundantly, and a large research and development lab near the company's headquarters in Rochester, New York, churned out incremental improvements to the core technologies for which the company was known. Yet something new was appearing on the scene that would change the world in which Xerox operated: computers. A few key leaders at Xerox recognized that computers were the force that would shape the future. Yet the established culture that pervaded the company, including at its own research facilities, was focused on designing and selling copiers. It had little use for computing. So Xerox decided to create a research facility far away from headquarters in order to pursue the innovation that the rest of the company didn't seem willing to embrace.

The Xerox Palo Alto Research Center (PARC) opened in 1970 in what would become the heart of Silicon Valley. It was staffed largely by a young generation of graduate students and emerging computer scientists, not established scholars and researchers in the field. The culture at PARC was decidedly different from the rest of Xerox. Weekly free-for-all meetings brought researchers together on bean bag chairs to take turns presenting their work in an atmosphere of open provocation and intellectual debate. Anyone—regardless of rank—could speak up, press each other to articulate assumptions, and issue challenges to what was being presented. The people who inhabited PARC were the kind of eccentric engineers who didn't fit very well in the buttoned-down culture of Xerox. PARC developed its own alternative culture of intense creativity, collaboration, and play. Together, they invented a stunning series of breakthroughs, including the personal computer, mouse, laser printer, graphical user interface, Ethernet, and many other innovations that most of us still use daily.

But Xerox largely failed to capitalize on these innovations. Steve Jobs and Bill Gates visited PARC, looked around, lured people away, and made far more use of what the PARC researchers had created than Xerox was able to. Today, Xerox is still largely known for making copiers. It missed out on the personal computing revolution that Apple, Microsoft, and so many other emerging companies profited from so spectacularly. PARC offers a rich parable of a major attempt to innovate within an established organization—an attempt that was, on the one hand, tremendous in the innovations it birthed, and on the other hand a colossal failure in terms of the established organization receiving these gifts.[1]

The PARC story is instructive for the church to consider as it seeks to embrace innovation. Currently, there are a variety of forms of experimental Christian community appearing across various faith traditions, such as Fresh Expressions and emerging churches.[2] Many established denominations have ethnic and multicultural congregations and ministries. These different forms of community represent vital attempts to recontextualize Christian life and practice within the diversity of cultures present today in the neighborhood. Many denominations and judicatories are authorizing pioneer ministries of various sorts in the form of church plants and alternative worshipping communities that bear little resemblance to established models. Local congregations are launching probes into their neighborhoods for the sake of connecting with their neighbors in witness and service. Such experiments are critical to learning our way into a new future. Yet many are also vulnerable to the same pitfalls that befell Xerox and PARC. How can innovation within established congregations and church systems be undertaken in mutually transformative and lasting ways?

Forgetting, Borrowing, Learning

The organizational scholars Vijay Govindarajan and Chris Trimble suggest three basic practices for new initiatives within existing organizations: *forget*, *borrow*, and *learn*.[3] Forgetting is about letting go of the assumptions, mindsets, and biases that dominate the status quo in the established organization. It is not easy to do, because organizations tend to be designed for ongoing operations, not innovation. Govindarajan and Trimble use the term "Performance Engine" to describe the established operations. Performance Engines are the existing way of doing things that bring in the primary income to the organization and define its dominant culture. They are the product of past success and they try to make every activity, task, and process as repeatable and predictable as possible.[4] For churches, the Performance Engine would be the existing mainstream membership, worship, programs, and ministries.

In order to innovate new forms of organizational life and practice, new competencies are typically required. Yet the dominant culture and patterns of organizations tend to be focused on established Performance Engine competencies, not new ones. Most organizations operate with the normalcy of trusted patterns that have been reinforced over time and experience. The culture buttresses this status quo and often suppresses the new. There is often an inherent tension between ongoing operations (the Performance Engine) and innovation. Without releasing some of these established assumptions, perspectives, patterns, and habits, however, innovation is impossible. We've been talking throughout this book about the importance of examining assumptions. At the heart of forgetting is the willingness to suspend, revisit, or alter basic assumptions by which we operate together.

New innovation initiatives must borrow from the established organization if they are to thrive. Borrowing happens on multiple levels. The most basic is resources—whether funding, people, facilities, community connections, or other assets. The blessing of innovating within an established organization is that you aren't starting from scratch; you have resources and momentum upon which to build. Wisdom, traditions, and practices all constitute treasures that can be shared with the new innovation that is emerging.

This borrowing and sharing must be structured and discerned carefully, however. It is easy for people in the established organization to be suspicious of resources being dedicated to something that might seem unfamiliar or threatening to them. Resentments can arise. In times of hardship, those resources can be withdrawn in a posture of hunkering down—often at precisely the moment in which the innovation offers the only promise of a way forward into the future. Typically, there is a power differential between the existing organization and the new innovation, leaving the innovation vulnerable to being undercut. Leaders must shape the community's conversation in such a way that there is widespread, shared knowledge of why the innovation is being undertaken and how it relates to the organization's mission.

For churches, this opens up great opportunities for longstanding values and commitments to be recast in ways that authorize innovation and change. For instance, if a congregation cares about passing its faith on to younger generations but is struggling to do so as children and grandchildren fade away from church participation, this core value could help. It would legitimize adapting new forms of Christian community and practice within the culture of those younger generations. Locating a useable past from which to borrow links the church's legacy and its emerging future in ways that foster the sharing of resources, authority, and wisdom.

Govindarajan and Trimble observe that experimentation is relatively easy, but learning is hard.[5] In other words, simply trying things out doesn't equate to lessons being captured and sustained for lasting change. They write, "Lessons are not magically revealed to those who have opened their minds with an experiment-and-learn attitude. Learning must be a conscious, explicit effort. It requires discipline. It requires accountability. And it requires a structured process."[6] Given the shame dynamics explored in chapter five, there is a natural human tendency not to talk openly about failures. It is tempting to keep experiments isolated, underground, or disconnected from the rest of the organization's life rather than make them public and participatory.

There must be regular cycles, practices, and spaces for action-reflection, which means convening conversations about what the Spirit seems to be leading the church to try in relationship with its neighbors, acting upon that discernment, and then coming together to discuss what went well and what we would do differently next time. Jesus's own formation of his disciples follows this pattern, as he sends them to try out ministry (see Matthew 9–10 and Luke 9–10, for instance) and then often debriefs with them afterward. The spaces for this kind of interpretation of experiments are critical; without them, the learnings are typically lost.

Action learning is how adults learn best—trying things out and then talking about what happened. Experience is primary here as we behave our way into new ways of seeing and being. Yet we must come together to reflect on what happened, or we are liable to lose the insights. Congregations may structure these reflection sessions in a variety of forms that fit their unique context and culture. They could be weekly practice groups, small groups, formal conversation spaces, or informal meetings over coffee or food. They can take place at church or in the neighborhood, but they must take place.

Integral to the process is the articulation of assumptions. Govindarajan and Trimble call this a "hypothesis of record"—a shared working assumption that is articulated formally by the group and then tested through experiments.[7] For example, a church's hypothesis of record in trying to connect with its unchurched neighbors might be that people are struggling to find meaning and community, but won't look to church to provide it. Therefore, the church must find ways to form relationships with these neighbors in their spaces that bring the Christian story and community to them. Along the way, the church will need to host what the authors call "Moment of Truth" conversations where they name the realities and evaluate the success or failure of the venture. There must be explicit naming of why we're doing what we're doing, what the experiments are teaching us, and the revised assumptions that set up the next round of actions. The church must ask the question, "What are we learning?" It is the only way for learning to proceed, since learning cannot be left to intuition alone.[8]

Partnerships for a New Future

Xerox failed to learn from PARC because it lacked a deep enough partnership between the existing operation (the Performance Engine) and the new innovations that were being developed on the other side of the country in Palo Alto. While PARC created a space in which the existing culture and its constraints were lifted, fostering lots of innovation and creativity, it was too disconnected from the rest of the organization for its lessons and gifts to be shared and received. While Xerox did profit from some of PARC's inventions, the big opportunity for learning and change it presented was largely missed due to lack of partnership. Perhaps most importantly, Xerox's corporate culture was never significantly influenced by PARC, so the posture of adaptation and creativity that flourished at PARC never took hold within the larger company.

How can churches organize themselves for innovation in ways that simultaneously allow space for the suspension of existing patterns and the emergence of new forms of Christian community, on the one hand, and foster deep ties to the established church, on the other? More than one innovative church leader has given up and bailed out in frustration after being so marginalized by status quo structures that she decides her voice will never be welcome. At the same time, many existing church members never feel like innovative forms of Christian community are accessible or comprehensible to them, so they disregard, dismiss, or denigrate them.

Herein lies one of the dilemmas of innovation. On the one hand, the innovation that we're exploring in this book involves adaptive learning that the whole community must own and share through participatory conversations and engagement. If it is left up to only some people, it will tend to be treated like a technical problem that others will solve for us; most people will feel they are off the hook and don't need to learn or change; and more widespread transformation and learning will not occur. On the other hand, not everyone is ready and eager to engage in innovative experiments. Some are far more willing to enter this work than others. This is why the disconnected approach that characterized Xerox PARC and characterizes so many experiments in

Christian community today is so common. It can seem easier to let the innovators go and do their thing without messing up the established organization; that way a truce is formed, turf is kept separate, and everyone is happy.

Yet this disconnected approach ultimately fails. There may be innovation, but it will likely not last, and the existing organization will not benefit from it. The established church will continue on its path, even as its future seems increasingly uncertain, while the fledgling forms of new Christian community struggle for viability. Leadership is crucial here. As we have been discussing, leadership involves creating a holding environment in which the big, adaptive challenges facing us as a whole are named and owned by everyone. These system-wide conversations in turn authorize the multiple spaces for small experiments in which responses to those challenges are innovated. People can then enter and embrace those experiments and their learnings at different paces.

Let's unpack this in more detail. Govindrajan and Trimble stress that the structuring of teams for innovation must be very deliberate. They urge that a *dedicated team* be created to take the lead on experiments, working closely with shared staff from the Performance Engine (established organization). The dedicated team should include outsiders, people marginal to the organization's established operations who can bring unique perspectives. The dedicated team must not be dominated by the cultural habits and assumptions of the Performance Engine. But it must stay closely connected to the Performance Engine through the shared staff and by including stakeholders from the Performance Engine.[9] This avoids the common problem of innovation initiatives being so marginal to the ongoing operations that learning doesn't take place in the larger organization. It provides for a fruitful polarity between those whose impulse is toward embracing the new and those bent toward conserving the past. The church needs both "treasures new and old" (Matthew 13:52).

Putting them into close relationship fosters innovation that is richly rooted in the tradition.

If innovation is going to spread within an existing congregation or community, it must be experienced firsthand in participatory ways—not just by innovators, but the larger population. Extensive research has been conducted on how innovations spread within human communities. This research documents that in any given community, only a small percentage (typically 2.5 percent) actually comes up with new innovations. These are embraced quickly by early adopters (who make up about 13.5 percent of the population) and more gradually by the early majority (34 percent) and eventually by the late majority (34 percent). Finally come the laggards (16 percent) who are most resistant to change, often for good reason.[10] The danger of isolating innovators and early adopters from the rest of the community is that what they learn will never spread and take hold without the participatory engagement of the majorities.

The research on diffusion of innovations reveals that it takes time for people to become aware of, understand, try on, and evaluate something new before they adopt it. There is simply no rushing this process. However, many innovators by nature grow impatient and ready to move on to the next thing. They should be allowed to. But if they are the only ones involved in an innovation process, there will be lots of interesting experiments that never land anywhere. Lasting change and learning will not take root, which is why the participation from early on of representatives of the majorities of the community is so vital. Stakeholders in the established legacy way of doing things should be directly involved in the experimentation and discovery process, but they should not be allowed to dominate it.

This is where the importance of a broader holding environment comes in. If we're having a public conversation as a community about the tough, vital questions for which we don't yet have answers, we begin to recognize that we're all in this together. We need each other's gifts, perspectives, and expertise. In this ongoing conversation, the discoveries and stories of the innovators and early adopters can be shared widely for everyone to learn from. At the same time, people can experience, evaluate, and embrace the new learnings at their own pace, and the wisdom of the laggards is kept in the conversation.

The key to the process of diffusing innovation is fostering experiential spaces for learning and trial. While there may be a small group of creative leaders who thrive amidst the dream of the new and the next, most people do not. They experience and interpret daily life within the framework of established routines, inhabiting a much more mundane comfort zone. In today's fluid society, there are so many changes and challenges being thrown at people as it is. They aren't looking for innovation and change from church, but rather stability and security.

People must be invited into relatively safe peer learning spaces of trial where they can concretely experience new ways of doing things. The idea is not to sell people on the latest idea about church, which they will likely dismiss as a fad, but rather to meet people where they are and try out embodied practices in which a new future is already present. People in the early and late majorities are willing to do this when they see peers experimenting with, embracing, and talking about new practices and habits. The research on diffusion of innovations indicates that peer learning through existing social networks is the primary means for spreading change.[11] This process takes time—a lot of time. There is no rushing it if the learning, innovation, and change are going to become long lasting.

For established churches and church systems like judicatories and denominations, these spaces of peer learning, knowledge sharing, and experimentation must be structured intentionally and authorized by leaders. Leaving them to chance or keeping them invisible, underground, and on the margins will not serve lasting transformation. At the same time, innovation must be undertaken in large part on the edges of the church's established life. The key is to create partnerships and communication loops by which what is being learned on the edges can inform the life of the center.

Precisely this kind of dynamic occurs in the book of Acts as the apostles are led by the Spirit into ministry outside Jerusalem among the Gentiles. In these encounters, disciples discovered vital new learnings about the gospel and the shape of Christian life and witness. For instance, the idea that Gentiles can join the community without first becoming culturally Jewish (through circumcision) wouldn't have likely occurred to the Jewish apostles in Jerusalem; it came from firsthand encounters with Gentiles in whom God's Spirit was at work. This idea required renegotiation of the established assumptions and norms among the Jerusalem church, which took place at the council described in Acts 15. Through the close network and connections between the mission on the edges and the mission in Jerusalem (the symbolic geographical center of the initial Christian movement), questions and learnings were shared through mutual dialogue and discernment.

For congregations and church systems, what are the means by which the innovative experiments and expressions of Christian community are being shared and diffused? One of the legacies of the establishment era is that local churches often operate in a competitive, rather than cooperative, posture toward one another. They are afraid of opening up their lives and learnings for fear that other churches might steal members, or that their own lack of competence will be exposed. The organizational structures that dominate judicatories and denominations tend to be designed for governance, control, and uniformity, not for innovation and peer learning.

The Role of Leaders in Innovation

What role should leaders play in learning and innovation within established churches and church systems, then? Remember Roxburgh's Rule? *To the extent to which the work of change is undertaken primarily by leaders, there will be no change.* Senior leaders cannot be the primary innovators. Their job is to tend the overall life of the community, including maintaining the Performance Engine, while at the same time legitimizing and creating space for innovation to take place through creating a holding environment. Let's unpack this in more detail.

In the face of adaptive challenges, people like nothing better than for leaders to shoulder the work of adaptive learning, thereby taking them off the hook from having to learn and change. It can be tempting for leaders as well to try to step in heroically with solutions to these challenges. But adaptive challenges by definition can only be addressed by learning and discovery on the part of everyone. So leaders must first refuse to take on the adaptive work of learning and innovation on their own, and instead engage ordinary members of the church in it. In the words of Ronald Heifetz and Marty Linsky, they must "give the work back to the people."[12]

Since adaptive learning is uncomfortable and involves loss, people tend to resist it, which raises another temptation—denial, or failing to have public conversations about the need to address the adaptive challenges. Everyone will be more comfortable if we simply maintain the status quo, right? People naturally look to leaders to relieve them of their fears of loss and to reassure them that everything will be fine. Leaders must refuse this path and instead help the community to interpret the realities it faces, as difficult as they may be, while inviting people into the practices and small experiments that open up a new future. Leaders should address people's learning anxieties by cultivating relatively safe spaces for shared conversation, trial, and discovery—a holding environment.

Organizational scholar Peter Block suggests that leadership in today's world should be about convening spaces for people to experience a new future together.[13] This task involves the relational work of bringing people together around areas of common concern and setting the table for good conversations about what matters most. In such conversations, the answers aren't predetermined. Difference and conflict can emerge in generative ways because the conversation space is defined by parameters of mutual accountability and trust. Leadership is about asking the questions for which there are no easy answers but which must be engaged if the church is to live into a new future. The very experience of having such conversations itself becomes a taste of that future, as voices are freed to name challenging realities and to draw on the treasures and wisdom of the past in addressing them.

This brings us to the *interpretive* dimension of leadership—the ways leaders help people make sense of reality. One of the primary roles for senior leaders in the process of innovation is to be public interpreters of the church's identity and calling in a changing world. Rather than imposing a vision unilaterally (and thus taking the work of discerning a communal vision away from the people), leaders are responsible for engaging people in the work of listening to God, to Scripture, to tradition, to their experience, and to neighbors.

Interpretative leadership entails cultivating intentional spaces for practices of listening, storytelling, and peer learning. It means inviting people across differences together into common spaces of deliberation and inquiry for the sake of discerning who we are in God, where we are in our context, and where God is calling us to go. The challenge is that many congregation members don't feel well equipped to interpret their life and experience theologically (i.e., in light of God's activity and presence). Leaders must use their own fluency with Scripture and tradition to guide people into these sources of the community's identity. It is less about periodic strategic planning processes geared to articulate aspirational mission statements and visions than it is about ongoing spaces for communal interpretation. When leaders help the church reflect upon its God-given identity and calling amidst a changing context, they create the public legitimacy for innovation.

Leaders can also assemble the dedicated teams who will take the lead on experimenting and reporting back to the wider community. This role may involve encouraging members of the church who don't see themselves as particularly innovative to participate alongside those who are eager for change. It is vital to create the feedback loops by which the congregation as a whole can know what is going on in these experiments and what is being learned through them. The work here is largely that of structuring communal life and relationships with an eye toward cultivating a shared conversation about learning and adaptation.

Since everyone is responsible for adaptive work, leaders must foster widespread participation, including lifting up a variety of voices and stories in the public conversation. This means protecting marginal voices (whether of innovators or of laggards). Those most eager to embrace innovation may feel at odds with the church's status quo culture and assumptions; their experience must be heard rather than suppressed, as it yearns for and begins to illuminate the shape of a new future. It is just as easy to denigrate and exclude laggards in the process of adaptation and change. Yet laggards don't want to abandon the past too quickly for good reason; often they are connected to meaningful treasures that should not be lost.

Leaders thus serve as architects of communal spaces of conversation, practice, and experimentation. Senior leaders in particular who hold formal authority (such as senior pastors or church board chairs) must remain connected to the full spectrum of the congregation's constituencies rather than identifying publicly with only a narrow band. Sometimes a leader will be most sympathetic with innovators and desire to spend most of her or his time directly in the work of experimentation and change. Yet doing so risks losing relational influence with the rest of the congregation, allowing oneself (and the innovation) to become marginal. Or a leader may personally be skeptically inclined toward the innovation and may feel more comfortable in the status quo. It is vital to be present to the innovators as well as the early adopters, majorities and laggards. Communities read leaders carefully for cues about what is important and legitimate.

If the ordinary members of the congregation are the frontline change participants in the power of the Spirit in this work, a central responsibility of leaders is to create, authorize, and tend the spaces in which it takes place, which may mean reordering how the church's life is structured to free up time and energy. Suspending ministries, committees, activities, or programs for which there is little energy in order to dedicate space for this work is vital. Most churches I know are doing too many things; the journey of innovation and agility will likely require simplification. This simplification is part of the pruning that Jesus talks about in John 15. New life and growth may depend upon a refocusing of energy, resources, and time.

Throughout the process, as the church's life and witness are adapted, translated, and reinterpreted, there are legitimate fears that leaders must address. People may wonder whether they are still welcome, whether their church is still there for them. The shape of their participation may change as expectations come to be redefined. This change is hard, especially for long-term members, because loss is involved. To the extent to which leaders can continue to love people, foster relationships among all members, and allow space for people to engage the work of discovery at their own pace, the community will hold together.

Not everyone may come along on the journey; recall that a generation died in the biblical wilderness. Yet when innovation is not leader-driven and coercive, when people don't feel like they are being managed into a future they don't understand or is uprooted from the past, and when they are given space to grieve losses and try things on at their own pace, transformation becomes a shared work. It is vital here to recall the Spirit's leadership, for it is precisely in the moments of crisis, despair, disorganization, and fear that God's Spirit forms new community in the Bible.[14] Leaders must help the community interpret its experience of innovation and discovery in light of the Spirit's movement. We aren't in this work alone. The agency isn't ours alone. The Spirit is ahead of us in the neighborhood inviting us to join in.

Innovation and Starting New Ministries

God's Spirit not only renews but also creates new expressions of Christian community, and the planting of new churches is a primary and often underutilized space for innovation.[15] New churches are typically more free to adapt their life and culture to meet people in the neighborhood than established churches with long and complicated legacies. They can embrace the cultures of new generations and populations from their inception, rather than trying to make space for them within an existing dominant culture. Life in new churches tends to be fluid and more flexible, not yet fixed into settled routines.

How might the insights we have explored so far in this book about innovation and agility inform how new churches are planted? In the past half century, there have been two predominant approaches to church planting in the United States. After World War II, as new suburban housing developments spread across America, denominations purchased land in those developments, hired a pastor to go door-to-door looking for the

Lutherans, Baptists, Methodists, Presbyterians, Episcopalians, and others moving in and invited them to join the new church. Plans for church buildings could be obtained from denominational offices, ensuring a fair degree of uniformity. The result was a denominational franchise paradigm for church planting based on the movement of existing Christians with denominational ties to new areas, who were then gathered into these new congregations. Many churches in American communities were founded this way. Needless to say, they are the product of a deeply establishment era.

Starting in the 1970s and '80s, a different model emerged, primarily among evangelical churches (and later copied by mainline denominations). This attractional or "seeker-sensitive" model was designed to reach the growing number of Baby Boomers who were estranged from the traditional churches of their childhood. Typically led by a charismatic founding pastor—Bill Hybels and Rick Warren being signature examples—these churches embraced contemporary entertainment, media, consumer, and business culture in order to try to connect with people in the neighborhood. Worship, programming, and all aspects of the church's life were geared strategically toward turning irreligious people into mature disciples of Jesus, to paraphrase Willow Creek Community Church's mission statement. Leaders envisioned a clear end product, and the church existed as an instrument to transform people into it. The goal was increasing church attendance and participation, with the assumption that the more actively involved people were in the church's life and programs, the more they were growing spiritually. Sophisticated marketing methods were employed to lure people in.

While this approach still functions in many places, it has come under scrutiny on several fronts. First, internal research within Willow Creek and other congregations using this model discovered that a basic underlying assumption was false—the presumed correlation between church program participation and spiritual growth.[16] Second, the model was largely predicated upon a particular age cohort—Baby Boomers—and its experience of church. Younger generations have been more resistant to the slick production values and corporate ethos of these churches. Finally, the missional church conversation has challenged the fundamentally church-centric vision at the heart of this model of church by arguing that the horizon of the church's ministry should be participating in God's mission to renew all of creation, not just getting more people into church.[17] Meanwhile, the leadership assumptions shaping the attractional approach to church planting tend to reflect a particular corporate managerial paradigm, where leaders set a vision and "align" people into it for the sake of implementation.

In this book, we've been exploring a very different paradigm of church life, practice, and leadership than either the established denominational franchise approach or the corporate attractional approach. In today's culture, it doesn't make sense for denominations to try to build new congregations by attracting their adherents who move into new suburban communities; there simply aren't enough adherents in most places for this to work, and denominational loyalty has deeply eroded. Yet it is remarkable how the franchise approach still dominates much denominational thinking and strategy around church planting. While this is beginning to change, new church starts are still typically measured according to the criteria of established churches, with the assumption that a "successful" result is a programmatic church that can afford a full-time pastor and staff and a dedicated building. This model of church is failing to connect with large portions of the people in our neighborhoods. Why do so many denominations tend to assume it should be normative?

In both of these models, the church typically begins with a leadership team who conceives of a vision for the new congregation, often apart from relationships and deep listening to neighbors who make up the "target audience." There may be demographic research on who is in the community, but the language of "targets" belies a tendency to objectify neighbors. The church focuses its energy on marketing itself to these people, not unlike any other organization vying for their attention, money, and time. Often there is a huge investment of resources from a sponsoring congregation, judicatory, denomination, or mission society to underwrite the endeavor.

These approaches make the same kinds of assumptions that traditional (rather than lean) startup companies make—they have a predefined product to sell, and once it is built, people can be invited into it through a big marketing push. The failure rate is not unlike that of traditional startups: very high. There are all sorts of theological and cultural assumptions at work here that warrant scrutiny. While leaders may indeed be inspired and led by the Holy Spirit in devising their plans for a church plant, the idea that they should do so in relative isolation from the neighbors God is calling them to form community with seems strange. In the New Testament, the Holy Spirit works *between* the apostles and the people they engage in witness and service and indeed is often out ahead of the apostles (as in Peter and Cornelius in Acts 10). The apostles don't typically understand what kind of witness God wants to bring forth until they are in the midst of it; it is much more improvisational.

When the church approaches neighbors like they are a target audience for marketing, it has reduced them from the genuinely other, immeasurably valuable, and intrinsically unique people God has created them to be, and turned them into objects. On some level, the presumption is that the church planters are in control. But in the New Testament, the apostles who plant new expressions of Christian community are hardly in control. That is why Paul's metaphor of "planting" is so rich. Any gardener or farmer knows that she cannot control the outcome of attempts at cultivation. Gardening involves all sorts of intentional activity—tilling the soil, fertilizing, watering, pruning, weeding, paying close attention to the environment. But God gives the growth (1 Corinthians 3:6).

How might the theological commitments and lessons on innovation we've been exploring in this book inform a different approach to church planting? First, church planters must begin with real openness to what the Spirit of God might want to bring forth, rather than starting with preconceived plans that just need to be implemented. In many neighborhoods, a church with a dedicated building, staff, and programming may not be the most fruitful embodiment of Christian community to connect with the people there. It is also not economically viable in many communities, especially if the church wants to be incarnate among immigrants, young people, and those experiencing poverty. Our imagination for what a legitimate new expression of local church might look like must become more expansive, without losing the core practices around which Christians gather: Word, sacraments, fellowship, witness, and service.

Church planting practice invites us into extensive conversations and relationships with neighbors in order to discern what God might be up to among the lives of the people in that place. This may mean convening discussions with community leaders and stakeholders about the neighborhood and its challenges and dreams, as the church publicly commits to seeking the neighborhood's flourishing (Jeremiah 29:7). When Christians present themselves as genuine partners in serving the well-being of the community, rather than just getting new members, deeper relationships, connections, and credibility open up. The gospel of Jesus is about God's gracious reign of justice and mercy coming into the midst of all. This authentic starting point can lead the church to collaborate with all sorts of community stakeholders to serve the common good. When neighbors observe that the church is dedicated to the neighborhood's vitality, not just its own, that becomes an integral dimension of witness.

If the Triune God—Father, Son, and Holy Spirit—is circulating around the neighborhood, we must attend carefully, patiently, and faithfully to how God is active and present in the lives of our neighbors. We must recognize God and our neighbors as acting subjects rather than objects. Church-planting teams are called to exercise deep discernment rooted in Scripture and the tradition as well as hosting ongoing conversations with neighbors, even and especially those who may never become part of the church. As we listen, we learn, which leads to "pivots" where our initial imagination about the shape of the new Christian community shifts in a different direction. Staying close to neighbors through small experiments and good failures from which lessons are gleaned is key to this work.

Epic Church in Fullerton, California, offers a vivid illustration of such a journey. Initially started as an offshoot of an established American Baptist church, Epic began as a small community of younger Asian Americans connected more through relationships than place. When they decided to move from south to north Orange County to be nearer members' homes and ended up in Fullerton, they had no idea what lay in store for them. Through settling into the heart of that city and forming community with the diverse people who live there—from shelter residents to aspiring artists and college students—God's vision for their church began to emerge. Instead of being a church of commuters, they grew into a church where increasing numbers of people walked to worship.

As they got to know key people in the community, doors opened. For instance, a newer member who has experienced homelessness and now works at the local shelter became a bridge person to the homeless community. The congregation has grown more racially, culturally, and socioeconomically diverse. Their listening to the neighborhood has led them deeper into local challenges, such as helping young people in the neighborhood to make it to college. At several steps of their journey, they have pivoted in response to their discernment of the Spirit's leading in relationship with neighbors.[18]

In today's cultural contexts, vital forms of local Christian community will take a diversity of shapes in order to connect with different populations, sometimes within the same neighborhood. The "one size fits all" approach of the traditional geographical parish, which held the promise of uniting everyone in one place across generational and socioeconomic lines, has never fulfilled its ideal in the midst of America's religious pluralism and choice. Its contemporary equivalent, the megachurch with market-segmented options for all, still misses many people. We live in a moment in which multiple forms of church will coexist, some small, some large, some with dedicated buildings, others without. This diversity invites us to rethink the economic model for many church plants. Already, there are new ministries being started in a variety of places around a business like a café, which serves as a public space of hospitality and community connection. Not only does this provide income, but it also offers a more accessible entry point for relationships than a traditional church building.

In Renton, Washington, a dying established Lutheran church was torn down and replaced by a new form of Christian ministry. In the new multiuse building, apartments for veterans are upstairs while on the street level is Luther's Table, a café, pub, neighborhood gathering spot, gallery, performance space, and worshipping community birthed and supported in partnership with another established congregation in the area, the local Lutheran synod, and the wider denomination. The café space incorporates elements from the old church, such as pews and stained-glass windows. It claims and carries forward Martin Luther's practice of holding "table talks"—conversations about God and life with colleagues, students, and friends. It is open, inviting, and accessible to people who would never enter a traditional church. Rather than receive tips, the café invites donations that support local community service ministries. This new church plant is meeting people in a profoundly unchurched area where they are, carrying forward elements of the past, and translating and opening up church traditions into expressions that people can enter into.

The church needs a plethora of experiments in nontraditional models in order to enter a new future. Yet those experiments must be connected to existing church communities, as we have explored above, for the learning to be harvested. Church planting is best undertaken in deep partnership with existing congregations. There is no innovation without collaboration. This should go beyond simply grants or funding to include participation by members of established congregations whenever possible, so that what is learned in the new ministry may be brought back to influence the existing one. When our emphasis is no longer on competing for scarce new members but rather seeking the peace of the city or neighborhood as participants in God's mission of reconciliation and renewal, we can discover common ground. Such a kingdom focus frees us to discern and affirm our distinct gifts while joining together, not only within denominations and church systems but also across them.

Reenvisioning Judicatory and Denominational Life for Innovation

Existing judicatory and denominational structures tend to embody an establishment, rather than innovative, posture. While many of them were birthed originally to serve missionary expansion, the past century has seen them embrace corporate bureaucratic and then regulatory agency approaches.[19] They have been geared to control the ministry within their purview, whether through licensing, credentialing, and deploying clergy, ensuring uniformity of policy and practice, redistributing resources, or legitimizing and delegitimizing particular expressions of local church life.

Some of this work is necessary to preserve the church's unity and integrity. Yet much of it inhibits innovation and learning by enforcing assumptions and standards from the establishment era. For instance, many denominational judicatories expect local churches and their leaders to fit a certain institutional model in order to be legitimate. Typically this means a dedicated building, a certain size membership, and a minimum salary and benefits package for clergy. Viability is measured against a particular (often implicit) model of a franchise establishment church. Those who don't fit this mode are then marginalized. Yet the demographic reality of many denominations and judicatories today is that the self-sustaining franchise church is becoming the exception, not the norm. It is unsustainable in many places.

In the face of the massive cultural shifts eroding religious participation and practice, the typical response is often to reorganize and restructure, sometimes by seeking to enforce norms and policies more assertively. Aggressive goals for church growth are set, to which judicatory leaders try to hold local leaders accountable. The assumption here is that we can manage our way into a predetermined future. People look to judicatory and denominational executives and staff to fix the decline and are disappointed when they don't. Sometimes, the language of "missional" or "innovative" is laid over old structures and practices without substantively changing the underlying imagination, which will always revert to the old defaults. All of this behavior is consistent with how organizations tend to react in the face of adaptive challenges. It simply doesn't work, however, because it never addresses the underlying cultural changes taking place.

Rather than trying to reorganize their way into a new future, judicatories and denominations might embrace a different posture. This posture begins with recognizing that the primary problems are not organizational or structural, but cultural; they have to do with basic ways of interpreting and experiencing life in the world among church members and neighbors alike. Mere organizational change will not address them. There are no clear destinations to manage our way into. At the same time, the future is already present in our midst, though largely unrecognized. The necessary learning and change must be undertaken primarily at the grass roots by ordinary disciples; it cannot be mandated and controlled by those in formal authority. Innovation involves a shift in imagination that comes through practices and participatory engagement with the biblical narrative; we live our way into new patterns through small experiments, rather than focus on dreaming up an aspirational vision far from today's realities. Such experiments require an environment of relative safety on the part of people doing them so that they are able to risk learning. Leaders are responsible for cultivating the spaces and stories for this learning to be experienced and shared—the holding environments for transformation.

For judicatory and denominational organizations used to seeing themselves as experts operating at the center of the church's life, this idea represents something of a paradigm shift. There is no "center" for the kind of learning and innovation the church must embrace; there are only countless small outposts. The local is the primary arena for this work, which is why many local churches find judicatory and denominational structures, agendas, assemblies, and programs irrelevant today. They are disconnected from the engagement that local disciples are called to undertake. The "experts" at the judicatory and denominational "centers" aren't particularly helpful because the answers aren't lodged there.

So what are these structures to do? To begin with, many existing denominational and judicatory committees and structures
have long outlived their usefulness. They can be pared down so
as to free up more resources (money, time, and energy) for local
innovation and collaboration. It is not at all clear yet what forms
of regional, national, or global organization will be adequate for
the twenty-first-century church, but corporate bureaucracy and
regulatory agency are not it.[20]

At the same time, if the primary challenge facing the church is
learning how to form Christian community and practice Christian
witness in a post-Christian society, judicatories and denominations can play a vital role in fostering shared learning. As learning
emerges from the grass roots, these structures can encourage peer
networks of communication and collaboration. Such collaboration cannot be legislated or mandated, but must come out of local
initiative to address shared needs. Often, local churches struggle
in isolation from one another. Judicatories and denominations
are connectional bodies. The shape of the connection may need
to change dramatically, however, if the purpose is mutual learning and innovation rather than regulation and uniformity. In this
work, judicatory and denominational executives cannot be the
primary innovators; their role is to foster spaces of practice, learning, storytelling, experimentation, and discovery—to convene and
connect rather than to control.

Sometimes, the new shape of regional connection might
emerge informally through network structures developed at the
grass roots. For instance, in western Massachusetts a group of
innovative ministries seeking to form community with neighbors estranged from established forms of church is linked
together through the Clearstory Collective. Reclaiming the early
church's network of small Christian communities as a model, the
Clearstory Collective includes ministries for college students, con-
templative worship gatherings, a community garden, pubs groups,

and worship in the streets. They are linked together for mutual support, learning, and resource sharing.[21]

Innovation and Theological Education

Patterns of leadership education in many denominations and church systems reflect the kinds of establishment assumptions that shape denominational and judicatory life as we've explored above. The system of ordination candidacy and education is largely driven by individual discernment (people are expected to present themselves with a call rather than be identified by local communities based on demonstrated gifts and behaviors), high barriers to entry (having a bachelor's degree and the capacity to undertake a lengthy and expensive seminary degree), and standardization (uniform seminary curricula and ordination examinations). Candidates are screened and molded primarily to fill existing slots in the system, not to change or adapt it. By the end of their navigation of a long and complex ordination process, including seminary, these leaders have typically been normed to the assumptions, expectations, behaviors, and patterns of the established church. Seminary education largely focuses on preparing graduates to fulfill expectations of existing members rather than cultivate new forms of Christian witness and community with those far from church. Whatever innovative impulses, imagination, and practices they may have brought with them into this process tend to be suppressed or even erased altogether by the end of it.

This approach to leadership development often fails to identify and form the kinds of leaders the church needs to discover a new future. It is typically inaccessible to those without significant financial resources or unwilling to take on high levels of debt amidst a shrinking pool of paid positions. It is difficult to navigate for those from cultures other than the dominant one, especially immigrants. It forces people to relocate to a residential seminary or to take a first job, removing them from the missionary contexts they know best. Few seminary faculty seem to have knowledge of or experience in the kinds of adaptive and innovative leadership required for the church today. In many respects, the whole system of ordination candidacy and theological education in many traditions is built for a world that is rapidly disappearing.

What can the church learn from its own past and from other fields about how to educate innovators? It is vital to recognize that the kind of centralized system of ordination and theological education that dominates many church systems today is not that old. For much of the church's history, including in America, leaders were largely educated through local apprenticeships under the supervision of experienced clergy. The complicated, bureaucratic candidacy processes of today's denominations emerged out of a professionalized paradigm for clerical leadership that came to prominence only in the mid-twentieth century. Every church tradition has elements of a useable past to discover in its own history of educating leaders.

Theological education isn't the only field in which a standardized, industrial-age educational system stands at odds with the kinds of imagination, behavior, and capacities required to lead organizations into an innovative future. The education scholar Tony Wagner conducted extensive interviews with younger innovators from a wide variety of backgrounds and disciplines—from an engineer who led the iPhone design team at Apple to a pioneering shoe designer from inner-city Memphis to social entrepreneurs addressing environmental problems and empowerment of urban youth.[22] What he learned offers fascinating challenges and opportunities for the church.

Three words summarize the growth of these innovators: *play*, *passion*, and *purpose*. Wagner found that the kind of play these innovators engaged in when they were growing up was often less structured than most children's, with ample space to experiment and discover through trial and error. It is precisely through this creative play that they discovered passion: something about which they cared deeply and which motivated them to learn and grow. Out of play and passion emerged a sense of purpose that led to their further development as innovators.[23] Their intrinsic motivation was rooted in curiosity and concern for the world around them.

One of the striking patterns in Wagner's interviews is how frustrating and alienating the established education system was for most of these innovators. The teachers and mentors who made the greatest impact in their studies were generally marginal to their educational institutions and made use of spaces outside the norm.[24] This was the case even with innovators who attended elite private schools and colleges. The key emphases for education innovators that Wagner discovered in his research are collaboration, multidisciplinary learning, the opportunity to create things, encouragement of intellectual risk-taking and trial and error, and intrinsic (rather than just external) motivation.[25]

Wagner discovered a couple of educational institutions that were breaking the mold in fostering innovative leaders. One was Stanford's Hasso Plattner Institute of Design (commonly known as the d.school), launched by David Kelley, a founder of IDEO (discussed in chapter four). Not only do students there have to solve a problem, they are asked to define it as well, which invites a deeper level of creativity and attention to the realities of the world. Yet the d.school exists somewhat uneasily within Stanford's larger culture, and this in a university known for its embrace of innovation. Many of the best faculty at the d.school don't fit into the usual academic categories because they blur the practitioner/researcher boundary.

Another unusual educational institution focused on educating innovators is Olin College, a small undergraduate engineering school in the Boston area with a student body that is nearly half female (unusual for engineering programs). Olin boasts a top faculty hired from places like MIT. What's different about Olin is that students are engaged in addressing real-world problems facing real organizations and businesses during their studies. They collaborate with these external partners in understanding the problems more deeply and improvising solutions. Throughout the undergraduate experience, the students work together in various hands-on capacities, sometimes embedded within actual corporations. Students graduate from Olin not only with a solid theoretical foundation in engineering, but also having already learned how to work together in real-world situations to solve real problems for which there are no easy answers.

What might these insights mean for the education of church leaders? While a fuller exploration of renewing theological education is beyond the scope of this book, let me highlight a few learnings. First, the kind of innovative leaders the church needs aren't always the ones who present themselves for formal credentialing in the established church. In fact, they may be those who experience themselves as estranged from the status quo yet deeply curious about and impassioned by the gospel. The church may need to identify these budding leaders and recruit them, rather than waiting for them to offer themselves to an ordination process that can feel discouraging. At the same time, some of those stepping forward for ordination may need to be redirected to other roles.

Second, theological education will need to meet people where they are, rather than expecting them to uproot from valuable missionary relationships and contextual knowledge in order to retreat to a monastery-like seminary campus far away. Theological education will have to take a variety of forms (as is beginning to become the case) to serve the needs of different leaders. Distributed learning and other formats will have to be utilized to bring the costs down and expand access. Gone are the days in which students could take on tens of thousands of dollars in seminary debt with the expectation that they would be able to pay it off through full-time ministry employment. Local churches, especially those engaged in innovative learning in their neighborhoods, will have to play a bigger role in leadership formation in partnership with seminaries and other institutions.

Third, the curricula and learning experiences of theological education must embrace real problems facing real churches and real people in the neighborhood through careful listening and exploration in relationship. The rich scholarly and intellectual traditions of Christianity should be brought to bear on these problems in dialogue with the wisdom of other disciplines of thought. Students must be empowered to try and fail in forming and restoring community with neighbors for the sake of the gospel along the way, and faculty and mentors must play a key role in this. New kinds of learning and expertise for faculty and staff involved in theological education will be required.

As with so many other forms of church life at the moment, it is not clear what patterns and shapes will emerge in different contexts to embody theological education and leadership development faithfully and adequately for an agile age. It will be through countless small experiments that this future becomes evident. There is much to borrow from in the church's history, legacy, and present. There is also much to forget—rules and norms that don't fit with the world we're in that should be suspended until better ones arise. And there is much to learn as we live together into the Way of Jesus under the Spirit's leadership.

Questions for
Discussion

1. Where is innovation currently taking place in the life of your church or church system?

2. How is that innovation connected to the rest of the church's life? How might it be more deeply connected?

3. What might need to be borrowed and forgotten for the sake of learning in your church?

Conclusion

This book has explored how God chooses and calls ordinary people like us into open-ended journeys of learning and discovery. These journeys are not intended merely for our own personal fulfillment but involve connecting with neighbors for the sake of sharing in God's healing of the world. In other words, God's healing of us doesn't end with us, but by its very nature links us in relationships with others. God's coming to us is also always a *sending* of us. As we have seen, these biblical journeys are not predicated upon our getting it all right, but rather on our willingness to trust in the One who claims and sends us and to be led by the Spirit of life, even if we are led far from home. The mistakes and failures that lie along these paths are integral to our growing up in Christ, not disqualifications from the journey. The church must renew its vision by more deeply inhabiting the central stories in which it finds its identity, even and especially amidst the dislocations of our contemporary world. It is fitting that we conclude this book by reflecting on one final biblical journey.

Being Joined on the Way

The Journey to Emmaus (Luke 24:13–35) begins where many church leaders and members find themselves today. Two disciples have left Jerusalem after their hopes and expectations have been dashed. They had believed they knew how the story was going to turn out—Jesus would restore Israel to sovereignty and prosperity. But the people had turned on him, their own leaders had betrayed him, and he had been crucified by the Romans. This is the worst imaginable ending. It is with grief, disorientation, and loss that they travel home to Emmaus, a place that likely no longer feels like home in the same way.

Jesus appears to accompany them precisely in this moment of lost hope and confusion. As with other Gospel stories, the resurrected Jesus is not easily recognizable, even to people who knew him. Resurrection is not mere resuscitation, but a deeper transformation; there is something genuinely new about this risen body. This is important to remember when we consider the death and resurrection local churches and church systems are undergoing. We cannot expect their life and form to look the same as previously. Innovation may bring forth new shapes for the body of Christ that may be difficult to recognize at first, even as they carry forward the life and marks (including wounds) of the past.

Jesus engages these two disciples with a simple question: "What are you discussing with each other while you walk along?" He meets them where they are, in their concerns and reality. Jesus listens them into speech, hearing their interpretation of the events that have just transpired in Jerusalem. Then he begins to help them reinterpret their experience and world through a different lens. Connecting what has happened to the biblical story of Moses and the prophets, Jesus invites them into a new imagination. He helps them make sense out of their situation using a common story.

As the day draws to a close and the disciples approach home, Jesus indicates that he plans to keep walking. Perhaps he doesn't want to impose himself upon them. But the two disciples prevail upon him to stay with them for the evening. It is only as they offer hospitality to him, sharing a meal together, that they come to recognize his identity and their eyes are opened to the deeper truth of who this stranger is. It is no accident that this recognition takes place in the breaking of bread. As in so many stories in the Bible, God's presence appears when bread is broken with strangers. Deeper connections open up in this sharing of hospitality, with all the mutual vulnerability it implies.

Even as the risen Jesus then vanishes from their sight, the two disciples find themselves reoriented. They recognize the passion they felt while Jesus walked with them on the road and shared the Scriptures with them, the burning of their hearts that comes with the change from grief to hope. This leads them to get up and go—even though it is night—back to Jerusalem to tell their companions what has happened. As Henri Nouwen observes, "Communion not only creates community, but community always leads to mission."[1] Having been joined on their way by Jesus, who in the exchange of story and hospitality sets them on a new path, they move from disorientation and despair to community and witness.

Churches today find themselves disoriented, grieving, confused, stuck, at a loss amidst the changing cultural realities of the twenty-first-century world. The ending hasn't turned out like we hoped it would in many places. We don't know what to do. We are like those two disciples. Like them, God has not forsaken us. Jesus draws near and accompanies us where we are, as we are. He inquires compassionately of us and challenges us to see things anew. As we break bread together at his table, we begin to recognize him in one another; our hearts burn with a renewed sense of purpose and hope. We are able to recognize that we too are sent to proclaim that he is risen to others.

Joining Others on the Way

In this story, we are the two disciples being joined by Jesus. But as the church we are also the body of Christ called to join our neighbors on their journeys of disorientation, loss, and suffering. We are called to accompany people where they are, as they are, and to inquire of them what it is they are discussing, how their hopes and expectations have been disrupted. We are called to listen them into speech and help them interpret their experience in light of God's story.

This is where Luke 24 must be put into conversation with an earlier story of sending, accompaniment and shared hospitality—the sending of the seventy disciples in Luke 10:1–12. The seventy are directed by Jesus to bear the peace into towns and villages by relying upon the hospitality of their neighbors, eating what is set before them and healing the sick. In being present in this way, traveling lightly, and sharing life together, they witness to God's reign come into their midst. The body of Christ must also being willing to eat at others' tables, to be the guest rather than just the host.

Learning and agility involve getting up and going, not just waiting for people to show up where we are. We must accompany them on their journeys, like Philip and the Ethiopian court official in Acts 8, inviting them to articulate their hopes, dreams, struggles, and fears. We are called to relate their stories to God's story, a story in which we discover our identities anew. We must seek spaces in which to break bread together, even at tables that are unfamiliar to us. In these encounters are often sacred moments. Sometimes we won't know exactly what words to say. We won't have quick answers to our neighbors' questions. What matters more is our willingness to go and to stay with them, to listen, and to share our own lived experience of the risen Jesus. This experience is embodied in our persons and relationships, in our words, and in our way of life.

Claiming the Promise

Innovation is about being made new. It is the heart of our identity as Christians. In Christ we are reborn (John 3:3–8), receiving a new identity that is sheer gift, an identity that joins us together with unlike people from every tribe and nation into a new community. The Spirit frees us from bondage to all that estranges us from God and one another so that we might share in God's restoration of the world. This renewal always involves loss—relinquishing the self-centeredness, control, and agendas that characterize the human condition in its fallen state. These things are put to death in us so that new life might emerge. There is no resurrection without death first.

At the end of our journeys lies a promise—that we are claimed eternally in a community of healing and mercy, sharing in a great feast at God's table. This promise frees us to take the risk of dying to all that keeps us from God and one another, trusting that new life will come forth. It frees us to enter into the lives and journeys of our neighbors as we share at their tables. It frees us to change, to grow, to learn, to fail, knowing we are held and carried by One who will not let us go.

Questions for
Discussion

1. When have you experienced God's presence amidst a time of disorientation and loss?
2. Which neighbors in your life and world might you be called to accompany on their journey?
3. How might the risen Jesus be present as you break bread together?

Notes

Introduction

1. See Pew Forum, "'Nones' on the Rise: One-in-Five Adults Have No Religious Affiliation," (Washington, DC: Pew Research Center, 2012); *www.pewforum.org/2012/10/09/nones-on-the-rise*.

2. Richard J. Foster, *Celebration of Discipline: The Path to Spiritual Growth*, rev. ed. (San Francisco: Harper & Row, 1988), 1.

Chapter One

1. Merriam-Webster Online Dictionary, accessed October 28, 2013, *www.merriam-webster.com/dictionary/agile*.

2. Oxford English Dictionary online, accessed October 29, 2013, *www.oed.com*.

3. Vijay Govindarajan and Chris Trimble, *The Other Side of Innovation: Solving the Execution Challenge* (Boston: Harvard Business School Press, 2010), 10.

4. See Alan J. Roxburgh, *Missional Map-Making* (San Francisco: Jossey-Bass, 2010).

5. Ibid., 125.

6. See Lamin O. Sanneh, *Translating the Message: The Missionary Impact on Culture* (Maryknoll, NY: Orbis Books, 1989).

7. Tim Brown, *Change by Design: How Design Thinking Transforms Organizations and Inspires Innovation* (New York: Harper Business, 2009), 17.

Chapter Two

1. Lesslie Newbigin, *Foolishness to the Greeks: The Gospel and Western Culture* (Grand Rapids, MI: Eerdmans, 1986).

2. This is a point made helpfully by Alan J. Roxburgh in *Missional: Joining God in the Neighborhood* (Grand Rapids, MI: Baker Books, 2011), 42–48.

3. Diana Butler Bass, "The Great Religious Recession," Mid-Winter Convocation, Luther Seminary, St. Paul, Minnesota, February 1, 2012.

4. Mark Chaves, "The Decline of American Religion?" ARDA Guiding Paper Series (State College, PA: Association of Religion Data Archives at The Pennsylvania State University, 2011), *www.thearda.com/rrh/papers/guidingpapers.asp*.

5. Pew Forum, "'Nones' on the Rise: One-in-Five Adults Have No Religious Affliation."

6. Jonathan Vespa, Jamie Lewis, and Rose Kreider, "America's Families and Living Arrangements: 2012" (Washington, DC: U.S. Census Bureau, 2013).

7. Anthony Giddens, *The Transformation of Intimacy: Sexuality, Love, and Eroticism in Modern Societies* (Stanford, CA: Stanford University Press, 1992), 49–64.

8. Zygmunt Bauman, *Identity* (Malden, MA: Polity Press, 2004), 89.

9. Anthony Giddens, *Modernity and Self-Identity* (Stanford, CA: Stanford University Press, 1991), 202.

10. Zygmunt Bauman, *Community: Seeking Safety in an Insecure World* (Malden, MA: Polity Press, 2001), 47.

11. Ibid., 14.

12. Charles A. Murray, *Coming Apart: The State of White America, 1960–2010* (New York: Crown Forum, 2012). Murray's discussion focuses on white America, but he demonstrates that trends in the collapse of marriage, family, labor participation, strength of religious affiliation, and happiness in lower-class America for whites and for the whole population track each other closely.

13. Ibid., 236–52, 285–95.

14. Robert Kegan, *In Over Our Heads: The Mental Demands of Modern Life* (Cambridge, MA: Harvard University Press, 1994), 152–53.

15. Ibid., 234.

16. Ibid., 185.

17. Charles Taylor, *A Secular Age* (Cambridge, MA: Belknap Press of Harvard University Press, 2007), 221–42.

18. Ibid., 223.

19. Miroslav Volf, *A Public Faith: How Followers of Christ Should Serve the Common Good* (Grand Rapids, MI: Brazos Press, 2011), 57–58.

20. Nancy Tatom Ammerman, "Golden Rule Christianity: Lived Religion in the American Mainstream," in *Lived Religion in America: Toward a History of Practice*, ed. David Hall (Princeton, NJ: Princeton University Press, 1997), 196–216.

21. Nancy Tatom Ammerman, *Sacred Stories, Spiritual Tribes: Finding Religion in Everyday Life* (New York: Oxford University Press, 2013), 45.

22. Volf, *Public Faith*, 57.

23. Ibid., 60.

24. Taylor, *Secular Age*, 299.

25. Grace Davie, *The Sociology of Religion* (London: Sage, 2007), 96.

26. Stefan Paas, "Mission among Individual Consumers," in *The Gospel after Christendom: New Voices, New Cultures, New Expressions*, ed. Ryan K. Bolger (Grand Rapids, MI: Baker Academic, 2012), 153.

27. Ibid., 154.

28. Ibid., 159.

29. The National Study of Youth and Religion; *www.youthandreligion.org*. Books based upon this study include Christian Smith and Melinda Lundquist Denton, *Soul Searching: The Religious and Spiritual Lives of American Teenagers* (New York: Oxford University Press, 2005); Christian Smith and Patricia Snell, *Souls in Transition: The Religious and Spiritual Lives of Emerging Adults* (New York: Oxford University Press, 2009); and Kenda Creasy Dean, *Almost Christian: What the Faith of Our Teenagers Is Telling the American Church* (New York: Oxford University Press, 2010).

30. Smith and Denton, *Soul Searching*, 31.

31. Ibid., 133. Mormons and conservative Protestants were most capable of articulating their faith, while Jews, Roman Catholics, and mainline Protestants had the hardest time doing so.

32. Ibid., 148.

33. Ibid., 155.

34. Dean, *Almost Christian*, 6.

35. Ibid., 30–31.

36. Ibid., 12.

37. Smith and Denton, *Soul Searching*, 171.

38. Charles Taylor uses the phrase "social imaginary" to describe "the ways in which [people] imagine their social existence, how they fit together with others, how things go on between them and their fellows, the expectations which are normally met, and the deeper normative notions and images which underlie these expectations." Taylor, *Secular Age*, 171.

39. Robert Wuthnow, *After the Baby Boomers: How Twenty- and Thirty-Somethings Are Shaping the Future of American Religion* (Princeton: Princeton University Press, 2007), 13.

40. Ibid., 120.

41. Ammerman, *Sacred Stories, Spiritual Tribes*, 298.

42. Ibid., 236.

43. See Elisabeth Kübler-Ross, *On Death and Dying*, reprint ed. (New York: Scribner, 1997).

Chapter Three

1. Allen Hilton, "Living into the Big Story: The Missional Trajectory of Scripture in Congregational Life," in *Cultivating Sent Communities: Missional Spiritual Formation*, ed. Dwight Zscheile (Grand Rapids, MI: Eerdmans, 2012), 82–93.

2. See Walter Brueggemann, *The Prophetic Imagination*, 2nd ed. (Minneapolis: Fortress Press, 1978).

3. Ibid., 6.

4. For a rich discussion of the importance of this passage for today's church, see Alan J. Roxburgh, *Missional: Joining God in the Neighborhood* (Grand Rapids, MI: Baker Books, 2011), 115–48.

5. Robert D. Putnam, *Bowling Alone: The Collapse and Revival of American Community* (New York: Simon & Schuster, 2000).

6. See, for instance, John D. Zizioulas, *Communion and Otherness: Further Studies in Personhood and the Church* (New York: T & T Clark, 2007); Stanley J. Grenz, *The Social God and the Relational Self: A Trinitarian Theology of the Imago Dei* (Louisville: Westminster John Knox Press, 2001); and Catherine Mowry LaCugna, *God for Us: The Trinity and Christian Life* (San Francisco: HarperSanFrancisco, 1991).

7. Jürgen Moltmann, "Perichoresis: An Old Magic Word for a New Trinitarian Theology," in *Trinity, Community and Power: Mapping Trajectories in Wesleyan Theology*, ed. M. Douglas Meeks (Nashville: Kingswood Books, 2000), 111–25.

8. Zizioulas, *Communion and Otherness*.

9. In the words of the Nicene Creed.

10. Roxburgh uses the phrase "language house" to describe the shared imagination in which we make sense of the world. See Roxburgh, *Missional*, 65–84.

11. Mark Chaves, *Congregations in America* (Cambridge, MA: Harvard University Press, 2004), 65.

12. Andrew F. Walls, *The Missionary Movement in Christian History: Studies in the Transmission of Faith* (Maryknoll, NY: Orbis Books, 1996), 7–9.

13. Newbigin, *Foolishness to the Greeks*, 4.

Chapter Four

1. Shoshana Berger, "The Emperor of Air," *Wired* (December 2012): 112.

2. Ronald A. Heifetz and Martin Linsky, *Leadership on the Line: Staying Alive through the Dangers of Leading* (Boston, MA: Harvard Business School Press, 2002).

3. Karen R. J. White, *Agile Project Management: A Mandate for the 21st Century* (Glen Mills, PA: Center for Business Practices, 2009).

4. Eric Ries, *The Lean Startup* (New York: Crown Business, 2011).

5. Brown, *Change by Design*.

6. Tom Kelley, *The Art of Innovation* (New York: Currency Books, 2001), 20.

7. Brown, *Change by Design*, 110–15.

8. Terry Jones, *On Innovation* (Lexington, KY: Essential Ideas, 2012), 55–56.

9. Chris Trimble, plenary address at Mid-Winter Convocation, Luther Seminary, February 6, 2013.

10. Clayton Christensen, *The Innovator's Dilemma* (New York: Harper Business, 2011), 3–26.

11. Ibid., 20.

12. Ibid., 178.

13. Ibid., 114.

14. Ibid., 241.

15. Richard T. Pascale, Jerry Sternin, and Monique Sternin, *The Power of Positive Deviance: How Unlikely Innovators Solve the World's Toughest Problems* (Boston: Harvard Business Press, 2010), 4.

16. All names of congregation members have been changed.

17. See Heifetz and Linsky, *Leadership on the Line*, 102–7.

18. Dwelling in the Word is a participatory practice of scriptural engagement that may be practiced as follows: A biblical text is read aloud while participants are invited to listen to where their imaginations were

"caught" or captured in the text. After a moment of silent reflection, participants pair up with someone to share what caught them or a question they would want to ask a biblical scholar about the text. When the larger group regathers, people are invited to share what their partner heard or wondered about. See *http://churchinnovations.org/06_about/dwelling.html*.

19. Dwight Zscheile, *People of the Way: Renewing Episcopal Identity* (Harrisburg, PA: Morehouse Publishing, 2012).

20. See Mark Lau Branson, *Memories, Hopes, and Conversations: Appreciative Inquiry and Congregational Change* (Herndon, VA: Alban Institute, 2004).

Chapter Five

1. See Heifetz and Linsky, *Leadership on the Line*, 102–7.

2. See Alan J. Roxburgh and Fred Romanuk, *The Missional Leader: Equipping Your Church to Reach a Changing World* (San Francisco, CA: Jossey-Bass, 2006).

3. C. Brené Brown, *The Gifts of Imperfection* (Center City, MN: Hazelden, 2010), 39.

4. Ibid., 1.

5. Chris Argyris, *Knowledge for Action: A Guide to Overcoming Barriers to Organizational Change* (San Francisco: Jossey Bass, 1993), 15.

6. Ibid., 50–55.

7. Robert Kegan and Lisa Laskow Lahey, *Immunity to Change: How to Overcome It and Unlock Potential in Yourself and Your Organization* (Boston, MA: Harvard Business Press, 2009).

8. Edgar H. Schein, *Humble Inquiry: The Gentle Art of Asking Instead of Telling* (San Francisco: Barrett-Koehler, 2013), 17.

9. Scott Cormode, *Making Spiritual Sense: Christian Leaders as Spiritual Interpreters* (Nashville: Abingdon Press, 2006).

10. Byungohk Lee, "Listening to the Neighbor: From a Missional Perspective of the Other" (PhD dissertation, Luther Seminary, 2013), 134–35.

11. See *www.frontporchaustin.org*.

12. See Lamin O. Sanneh, *Translating the Message: The Missionary Impact on Culture* (Maryknoll, NY: Orbis Books, 1989).

13. See Eddie Gibbs and Ryan K. Bolger, *Emerging Churches: Creating Christian Community in Postmodern Cultures* (Grand Rapids, MI: Baker Academic, 2005); Ryan K. Bolger, *The Gospel after Christendom:*

New Voices, New Cultures, New Expressions (Grand Rapids, MI: Baker Academic, 2012).

14. Peter Drucker, *The New Realities* (New York: Harper and Row, 1989).

15. Frank Barrett, *Yes to the Mess: Surprising Leadership Lessons from Jazz* (Boston: Harvard Business School Press, 2012), 2.

16. Ibid., 122.

17. Ibid., 123.

18. Ibid., 43.

19. Ibid., 12, 17, 61.

Chapter Six

1. See Michael A. Hiltzik, *Dealers of Lightning: Xerox Parc and the Dawn of the Computer Age* (New York: HarperBusiness, 1999).

2. See *www.freshexpressions.org.uk* and Gibbs and Bolger, *Emerging Churches.*

3. Vijay Govindarajan and Chris Trimble, *10 Rules for Strategic Innovators: From Idea to Execution* (Boston: Harvard Business School Press, 2005).

4. Govindarajan and Trimble, *Other Side of Innovation*, 10–11.

5. Govindarajan and Trimble, *10 Rules for Strategic Innovators*, 91.

6. Ibid., 93.

7. Govindarajan and Trimble, *Other Side of Innovation*, 134.

8. Ibid., 104, 35.

9. Ibid., 27–95.

10. See Everett M. Rogers, *Diffusion of Innovations*, 5th ed. (New York: Free Press, 2003), 281.

11. Ibid., 301–64.

12. Heifetz and Linsky, *Leadership on the Line*, 123–39.

13. Peter Block, *Community: The Structure of Belonging* (San Francisco: Berrett-Koehler Publishers, 2008), 85–86.

14. Michael Welker, *God the Spirit* (Minneapolis: Fortress Press, 1994), 56.

15. For an excellent recent resource on this topic, see Mark Lau Branson and Nicholas Warnes, eds., *Starting Missional Churches: Life with God in the Neighborhood* (Downer's Grove, IL: Intervarsity Press, 2014).

16. Greg Hawkins and Cally Parkinson, *Reveal* (South Barrington, IL: Willow Creek Association, 2007).

17. See, for instance, Craig Van Gelder, *The Ministry of the Missional Church* (Grand Rapids, MI: Baker Academic, 2007), 70–88.

18. See Kevin Doi, "Balancing Location and Relationships: Epic Church," in Branson and Warnes, *Starting Missional Churches*, 48–65.

19. Russell E. Richey, "Denominations and Denominationalism: An American Morphology," in *Reimagining Denominationalism: Interpretive Essays,* ed. Robert Bruce Mullin, and Russell E. Richey (New York: Oxford University Press, 1994), 74–98.

20. For an example of one denomination's exploration of these issues, see Winnie Varghese, ed., *What We Shall Become: The Future and Structure of the Episcopal Church* (New York: Church Publishing, 2013).

21. See *www.clearstorycollective.org.*

22. Tony Wagner, *Creating Innovators* (New York: Scribner, 2012).

23. Ibid., 26–30.

24. Ibid., 152.

25. Ibid., 184.

Conclusion

1. Henri Nouwen, *With Burning Hearts: A Meditation on the Eucharistic Life* (Maryknoll, NY: Orbis Books, 1994), 76.